Lessons In Our (early) 30s

Libby John and Jillian Kaiser

Dedication

To friends that have conversations that change the world!

One of the most beautiful qualities of true friendship is to understand and to be understood.

—Lucius Annaeus Seneca

Table of Contents

About This Book

Lessons in Our (Early) 30s is a book highlighting the lifestyle of the single woman in her early thirties with a focus on self-improvement. It is enlivened with personal experiences from the authors and compares current behavior and expectations with those of their former twenty-something selves.

Today's thirty-somethings are reaching for success in many life categories once they graduate from their twenties. More women are taking the time to "figure it all out" than did previous, more traditional generations and have a different order of priorities and concerns. Plenty of books document and advise the twenty-something woman on being her best self, assuming that everything will have been figured out at the start of her fourth decade—but not so! This book fills that gap by covering the major topics present in a woman's life including beauty, wellness, finance, career, fashion, romance, and spirituality.

One of this book's innovations is the thorough integration of social media: frequent hashtags in every chapter encourage the reader to directly interact with the authors, creating a sense of community. Readers quickly understand that they are not alone, drawing inspiration and camaraderie from the authors' stories, as well as guidance in avoiding a few of life's mistakes along the way. The authors of Lessons in Our 30s are long-time friends currently "figuring it all out." They are living through this era and realize that the journey can be confusing and exhilarating, a journey that motivates them to share their knowledge in an entertaining and powerful manner.

Howdy

It All Began With A Conversation . . .

"**W**hat the heck happened to you? You almost missed happy hour," Jillian asked. "I left work late to do damage control after sending my resume to my entire department. Then, I broke a heel running to catch this happy hour special since I only have ten dollars to spend. Good thing I'm wearing my Fitbit!" Libby exclaimed. "Wait . . . how is my hair? I'm having dinner here later with that guy I met online. Please, God, let him be The One!" We are sure every girl has a similar story!

This is how many of our conversations played out for the last eight years. However, this past year, we realized having meaningful chats can be rare, and we wanted to share ours with you, the reader. It's not every day that we find true friends who are open and honest with us, especially with no filters where anything goes when it comes to conversations.

We decided to create this book after one too many discussions about dating for marriage, career goals, and how cool it would be to lose ten pounds with one yoga pose. All of these talks carried more weight once we hit our thirties, and the idea that "we should write a book!" was born.

Our mothers walked five miles in the snow to fetch water, then cooked for the whole family, and were married with children by twenty-five. While they are chock-full of advice—whether we asked for it or not—they cannot fully guide us through the beginning of this new decade. They didn't have to worry about a profile picture online!

Introducing Libby And Jillian, Two Texan Authors

Libby: When I was growing up in the '80s, I loved Girl Talk, a game for teenage girls about topics such as having parties, talking on the phone, and of course, boys. Being an only child, I just always wanted to chat; I had something to say about everything, and Girl Talk gave me topics I never knew about. It was like Google without a modem (back-in-the-days talk).

Fast forward a couple of decades, and I finally got a computer with Wi-Fi, cable TV, and a real job after college in which I earned, saved, and spent money. I had it all! The next step was to meet Prince Charming, get married, and have a small white Maltese or Westie to start growing our family. Sounds so simple. But why is it so challenging, and why has it still not happened? That's what life is all about: the challenges. And when there are challenges, no matter what, your true friends (Hi, Jillian!) are always there with advice and support-- and maybe a margarita or two-- because they might be going (or have gone) through the same life events as you.

Jillian: I grew up in Houston, Texas, in the '80s and '90s, and like most of you, set out on the traditional path of college and career. Not being taught that marriage and kids should be a focus, it became an afterthought that would just "happen." So in my early days, I expected to be some fancy briefcase-carrying lady sashaying around, looking important. I couldn't wait to be an adult so I could do adult-like things. I thought twenty-five was old! Now, after so many years of learning, I have a great perspective on life, plenty of experience, and have never actually sashayed. I'm OK with that. I've made awesome friends along the way (Hi, Libby!), traveled far, and listened closely. There are still plenty of journeys planned for my life including marriage, children, and leaving a positive imprint on the lives of others. Most of all, I want to continue to enjoy this special time in my life and be the best thirty-something I can be.

The Book

It has been a fun journey navigating through our early thirties thus far. It's different from the twenties, but in many ways, the same. And instead of thinking it's the end of the world—as many ladies fear—we actually found it to be the exact opposite. It's Adult Part II and has its own teachings. Here's a quick lesson to get you going.

We still don't have it all figured out. And that probably won't change until Lessons in Our (Mid) 60s debuts. The last time we even thought we had it all figured out, Brenda was dating Dylan. That's the beauty of it all. You get to live, learn, and make fun memories about all that living and learning. Some are only enjoyable in hindsight, but you take something important away from each experience in your life. Everything happens for a reason! The realization that so many ladies were stepping into their thirties with our same hopes and fears inspired us to share our own experiences and be your best friends for the next nine chapters.

Through our book, we hope you, the reader, see us as your friends. Each chapter will provide our personal experiences, actions plans, tips, and lessons learned. We have also included a gazillion hashtags. This will allow you to connect with our Instagram account as you read through the chapters. We also encourage you to use the same hashtags to connect with all readers of the book and us. We are so excited to see your photo(s) and show you our pictures as well. Try it out! Here is the first hashtag: #lessonsinour30s.

This book has an intentional structure in which the nine main chapters are the building blocks of life. People naturally remember what a person looks like before remembering their name. It's the true first impression.

Most of us start our day by looking in the mirror ("Mirror, Mirror ..."). Then comes our strong body: it completes the picture of who you are ("Hey, Good-Looking"). To maintain our health and well-being, we develop nutritional habits ("Chow Time"). As reward to all the hard work, next comes the fashion show ("Style Me")

Money is the link that that ties everything together in life ("Money Magic"). We earn our first paycheck through our career ("Boss Woman"). Through these experiences, we gain and lose friendships ("My Contacts"). Finally, we meet that best friend who becomes our hubby, starting the union of our lives ("Love Story"). As a bonus chapter, it's through our belief that anything is possible ("Ask, Believe, Receive"). The titles are hyperlinks to our Instagram account and contain photo collages for a sneak peak of the upcoming topics in the chapters.

Throughout these major areas in life, we learn lessons and have experiences that are made to share with others. Welcome to Lessons in Our (Early) 30s! What matters for now is that you know that we get you. We are you. And for those of you in your twenties trying to get a leg up on your thirties that's so genius. Let's read on . . .

#MirrorMirror

*For attractive lips, speak words of kindness. For lovely
eyes, seek out the good in people. For a slim figure,
share your food with the hungry. For beautiful hair,
let a child run his fingers through it once a day. For
poise, walk with the knowledge that you'll never walk
alone. The beauty of a woman is not in a facial mole,
But true beauty in a woman is reflected in her soul It is
the caring that she lovingly gives, the passion that she
shows, And the beauty of a woman with passing years
only grows.*

—Sam Levenson, *"Time Tested Beauty Tips"*

How many selfies does it take before you get the perfect one? We can take about five before giving up and resuming shopping in Target's beauty aisle. Don't judge. You might notice that now your face is a little different in pics when compared to your twenties. Before we discuss the many facets of aging, let's take a minute to bask in our beauty. An Allure magazine study showed that women believe their peak beauty age is around thirty-one years. So if you were thinking your best days were in your twenties, we just dropped some knowledge on you. You are naturally looking your best, and all you have to do is prolong that title of Most Beautiful Right Now. The good news is that you probably have the least amount of selfie retakes #SelfieTime The sections below will guide you through everyday beauty tips, tricks, and advice.

Immortality Or Close Enough: The Goal Of Looking Ageless

Once we say goodbye to our twenties, we become aware that we're not young or old. It's a wonderful place to be because the external stressors of that era are fading. We are coming into ourselves, discovering that we're our own best friend. Our faces and bodies should reflect this transformation.

All those sleepless twenty-something nights with excessive alcohol, cigarettes, and sun have found their way to our face, neck, and chest. We are due for a change. The symptoms of these bad habits are not part of the natural aging process and can be managed. The bottom line: it's time to create more good habits and give bad ones the stink eye. And yes, we had regimens in our twenties, but now we're into the stronger stuff.

As product junkies, we love having an excuse to buy more promises in shiny little boxes. Sometimes we are more consistent with our routines than the brand, but we realize the importance of establishing a regimen to age gracefully like Cindy Crawford and Tyra Banks.

The common signs of aging are the following:

- Hyperpigmentation
- Fine Lines
- Slower Cell Turnover
- Dryness
- Dull Skin
- Loss of Elasticity

- Facial Volume Loss
- Dark Circles Under the Eyes

#FunInTheSun

Fun in the sun catching up with you? We all know and love the sayings about embracing wrinkles and calling them wisdom lines and experience catchers. We just made that last one up, but it sounds cool. Then you spot the picture online of the eighty-year-old monks who never see sunlight. Yep, they look seventeen years old and at peace with life. About ninety percent of our fine lines and wrinkles are from photoaging. That means the wise ones are protecting themselves from it. The real focus here is on practicing good sun habits by wearing more hats and a broad spectrum sunscreen with an SPF of at least 30 when you're exposed to UV light. For now, this is as close to a miracle in a bottle as we'll get!

Libby's Experience: I rarely spend time in the sun because I don't like buying new foundation and powder. It is so hard to match my skin tone. My doctor told me I have an iron deficiency and should spend time in the sun without sunscreen to get the adequate sunlight exposure needed to process vitamin D. I decided that thirty minutes was not enough time and stayed out for an hour and a half. You guessed it! I got sunburned! I didn't realize it until I felt a painful burning sensation on my legs and arms during my Hot Yoga class. Needless to say, I was prescribed topical medications and tons of aloe vera to heal my skin. Nowadays, I make sure to wear sunscreen and sometimes even a baseball cap when I go out in the sun.

Sunscreen Reminders

- Sunscreen for Face: Don't rely on your makeup for sun protection even if it has SPF.
- Sunscreen for Body: Use a daily body lotion with SPF from brands like Aveeno and Supergoop, so you never leave home without it.

Face Time

Washing and caring for the canvas that is your beautiful face is the foundation for your foundation. See what we did there? Nowadays, we should embrace a multipronged approach to keep our skin in order. Try gentle cleansers, and don't be afraid to use an oil-based solution to remove the makeup and pollution first. Double cleansing is great after a long night out. If you are into layering products, look for a toner with anti-aging benefits before moving onto your antioxidant rich serum.

Some of the most popular skin care products are listed below:

- **Retinoids**: A type of vitamin A that increases cell turnover and collagen. Available by prescription. Retinol, a milder version, is available over-the-counter.
- **Ceramides**: Help create a barrier of moisture for your skin and allow it to recover from sun damage and dryness.

- **Antioxidants**: Fight harmful free radicals to protect collagen and elastin.
- **Hyaluronic Acid**: Plumps skin by attracting about one thousand times its weight in water. Repairs skin affected by dryness and the environment.
- **Alpha Hydroxy Acids**: Slough off dead skin cells, fade age spots, hyperpigmentation, and fine lines.

Jillian's Experience: I am the queen of blackheads! After so many years of haphazardly addressing the issue, they have become more noticeable. I have an oily lowercase and uppercase "T" zone which makes me more susceptible to blackheads, so the battle constantly rages on. I started using a prescription retinoid when I turned thirty-two to keep my skin from being clogged, and it has really made a difference. The days of using Noxema and your mom's Oil of Olay are a distant memory. If you can build a modest but powerful arsenal of products to consistently protect your skin, you'll begin to notice wonderful things happening after just a few weeks.

  Libby's Experience: I always had acne issues growing up. The stress in my twenties and my lack of a daily face washing routine did not help. I tried multiple sensitive-skin products at Sephora to help but would use them for week or less, so I never saw improvements. Once I started getting facials, I was informed by the esthetician that relying on cleansers was not enough. I also needed toner and eye creams to see results. Remember to always ask for samples, so you save money before you commit to the products. I now have strict morning and evening routines when it comes to my skincare, especially since everyone is taking selfies without makeup #freshface! I can honestly say these changes, coupled with better eating habits, renewed my skin. More on the eating habits in the Chow Time chapter.

#MakeupGameOnPoint

The best thing is to look natural, but it takes makeup to look natural.

—Calvin Klein

How can something that makes us late for work, dates, parties, and life in general be so beneficial and fun? Makeup has much more meaning and pleasure once you're in your thirties because you begin to understand why less is more. Bobbi Brown, who started her makeup brand at thirty-three years of age, championed the "your skin but better" movement, and now is the time to participate in it. We should be leaning toward a natural-looking glow that works for us and manages the signs of aging we are not quite ready to embrace.

The following tips apply for all skin tones. Here's how to enhance what you've got:

- **Contouring and Highlighting**: It's not as scary as you think! Find a bronzer or contouring palette a few shades darker than your skin and blend it under the cheekbones. Blend it like you mean it. For highlighting, place it along your brow bone and the high points of your face. The benefit is an instant "lift" to compensate for the loss of elasticity.
- **Concealer**: Have a concealer on hand that matches your skin's tone for under the eyes. It's popular to purchase this product a few shades lighter than your skin tone to create a luminous effect, but it can end up illuminating wrinkles in the process.
- **Brow Fillers**: Remember our twenties when over-tweezing was in? Did your brows ever recover? Aging also reduces brow thickness and makes us look older than we are. Neat, full brows give you a youthful appearance and frame your face.
- **Eye Shadow**: The smoky eye has only been mastered by a few talented souls. This is the time to buy those quality brushes and watch YouTube tutorials until you (finally) get it right.
- **Foundation**: They don't have to be pricey. A Beauty Balm (BB Cream) or Color Corrector Cream (CC Cream) is great for everyday wear. Try a pigment-based foundation that can be

mixed with your sunscreens and serums. If you are darker in the summer, you'll need a matching shade; and don't forget to include your neck, so you don't look like a floating head in pictures.

- **Red Lipstick**: Experiment with both orange and blue undertones. We are still experimenting as well!
- **Mascara**: Our lashes start to diminish as we age, and if prescription growth formulas ain't your thing, you're best bet is great mascara.

Five Minute Face

1. Multipurpose foundation (BB or CC Cream) 1.0 min
2. Eyeliner and Mascara (no wings here) 1.0 min
3. Powder 0.5 min
4. Blush or bronzer 0.5 min
5. Brow filler and groom 1.0 min
6. Nude lipstick 0.5 min
7. Blend, smooth, perfect 0.5 min

Ten Minute Face

1. Primer 1.0 min
2. Multipurpose foundation (BB or CC Cream) 1.0 min
3. Eyeshadow (one or two colors) 1.5 min
4. Eyeliner and Mascara (small wings only!) 2.0 min
5. Under Eye Brightening and Spot Covering Concealers 1.5 min
6. Powder 0.5 min
7. Blush or bronzer 0.5 min
8. Brow filler and groom 1.0 min
9. Nude lipstick 0.5 min
10. Blend, smooth, perfect 1.0 min

Ready For Fillers And Injectables?

Nope. See Lessons in Our (Mid) 30s (coming soon). But do visit a dermatologist or aesthetician. They are experts in skin care and can guide you toward the best products for your face and body. Most of us go it alone because stores such as Sephora are cure-alls, but you are missing out on discussing additional options with a trained professional. They will also come in handy when you're ready to entertain more invasive anti-aging procedures. Again, we really don't recommend drastic procedures now and will never be quick to do so. We are currently on Team Love the Skin You Are In.

My Hair

Aside from having a few grays, most of us haven't experienced any traumatic differences. Okay, okay, finding gray hairs can be traumatic…However, now is the time to get the best haircut you can afford and easily style. Try a longer, styled cut with layers that complement the shape of your face. If you're afraid of bangs, now is a great time to end your fears and try them for a more youthful and playful look. Keep your ends neat with regular trims. Sometimes the difference between healthy looking hair and blah hair is cutting an inch off the bottom. Most importantly, give yourself an extra ten minutes in the morning to get it right each day. Not just on Thursday or when you know that cute guy will be there. Every day! This is a major step to looking polished.

To keep it hair-commercial-ready, start doing the following:

- Deep condition at least twice a month: Leave it on for minimum of thirty minutes and then shower and shampoo to keep from weighing your hair down.
- Don't be afraid of oil: Try a very light application of coconut, almond, or jojoba oil on your ends to revitalize the oldest, most fragile part of your hair.
- Sleep on a satin pillowcase: The friction and subsequent breakage from cotton pillow cases can slowly degrade your hair.

- Try a suds-free shampoo: It keeps your strands from fading and helps with dryness. If you cannot get used to the whole "no lather" thing, then opt for sulfate-free with an order of suds.
- Use less heat: When people tell you your hair looks better naturally wavy, believe them.
- When using heat, apply s on a blow dry spray with a heat protector to reduce drying and frying time.

Over the past few years, there has been a push to remove the chemicals in our hair products that do more harm than good. As we mentioned above, sulfate and sulfate-like products can fade even your natural hair color. With all of the hair care brands competing for your loyalty, it's important to choose the solution that cleanses, not strips, your strands. Read the labels. Here are some common ingredients to avoid: sodium laurel sulfate, propylene glycol, parabens, formaldehyde, triethanolamine and diethanolamine, imidazolidinyl and diazolidinyl urea. Before you purchase check for more potentially harmful ingredients by Googling them on the spot. If you can't spell it, why buy it?!

My Body

It's easy to take the rest of our body for granted as we coddle our faces. But those limbs and torsos need love, too! Start with exfoliating by using a long, soft brush or sugar scrub. Use a moisturizer that contains sunscreen and vitamins during the day and a thicker non-sunscreen formula at night.

Jillian's Experience: As a frequent wearer of sandals and flip-flops, I have to grab for the coconut oil and old socks monthly to keep my feet from Fred Flintstone-ing. I wear the combo at night to keep them soft and sandal-ready in the morning. Works like a charm!

My Beauty

We are definitely in favor of looking our best, but remember that loving and valuing ourselves will go deeper than rituals at any age. We had no problem telling others our age when we were twenty-nine or younger. But as soon as the big 3-0 hit, we cloaked our age in secrecy and hoped no one asked. There is beauty and favor in youth, and admitting we are no longer a part of that crowd can be difficult at first. In addition, we are conflicted between society's message to accept women as we are and participate in costly, painful procedures involving masks and lasers. It behooves us to understand that opportunities emerge when presenting our finest selves to the world. But since this transformation is just beginning, we must use the power of our own beauty. That thirty-something type of beauty that makes you content in your own skin and thankful for each birthday. Have fun with it, take care of yourself, and just do your thing.

LESSONS IN OUR 30S: (OUR FAVORITE BEAUTY SECRETS)

1. Freeze your eye liner for fifteen minutes so that it will glide seamlessly.
2. Massage an ice cube over your face until it melts. Do it every night before bed and keep fat cells, acne, and wrinkles under control.
3. Start dry brushing your body. Dry brushing is our favorite method of body exfoliation because it's multitasking—it's incredible as a cellulite treatment and increases elasticity.
4. If you're out of makeup remover, use body lotion to get rid of makeup. It works well on mascara!

#HeyGood-Looking

*L*ibby's Experience: I'm sitting on the couch Monday night after a long day of work, catching up on the latest episode of *Scandal*. As the drama heightens on the screen, my only thought is, "Where did Olivia Pope find that dress?" It's the perfect hunter green. I need that dress. I Google the details on the outfit and find the best deal on the Internet, but wait . . . what size am I? I typically wear smalls, but just last week I wore a size six dress. It looked absolutely amazing on me, but there is no way I'm a six when more than half of my closet contains size two dresses. Size two it is! Fast forward to the end of the week. Thanks to Amazon Prime shipping, the outfit has arrived. I rush to try it on, but it's a little too snug. As I carefully examine the situation in a full-length mirror, I see that all I need to do is lose a couple of inches here and there, and then the dress will fit perfectly. The revelation begins the "I need to lose weight" mantra. I know I'm not the only one who goes through this dilemma weekly.

Jillian's Experience: I never really had any weight goals until I was about thirty-one years old. I had been a size two since college and didn't think about pounds or inches. I ate whenever and whatever I wanted for every meal. Jack in the Box and Whataburger were my best friends. Then, seemingly out of the blue, my wool pants developed wear marks on the thighs and fitted skirts and dresses would bunch around my hips. Every few steps I would have to stop walking, pull my clothing down, and start again. I got so good at adjusting my clothing that I could do so while walking and not think much about it. It wasn't until I caught a coworker performing the same telling movements on her ill-fitting skirt that I decided to make some changes. I realized that other people could see my struggle, and it was like silently admitting there was an obvious, fixable flaw in my appearance. I might as well start wearing lipstick around instead of on my lips while I was at it! Since I did not plan on buying a whole new wardrobe, I knew, like Libby, I had some work to do.

Hello 30 Something Body

The lesson is that we're not in our twenties! Our health is still the most important part of our lives and should be a priority now more than ever before.

Here's what's happening to our thirty-something bodies:

- **Weight Gain.** Extra weight will begin to creep up and show itself in places you didn't expect. Think stomach, thighs, back, arms . . . OK, everywhere. The extra weight shows up everywhere! Our shape changes as we age, and in our thirties we have a fuller hourglass shape and/or more overall roundness. You can thank your slower metabolism.
- **Bone Loss Begins**. The road to osteoporosis starts now. Your bone mass starts to dwindle at a faster rate that it's being replaced.

- **Muscle Tone Fades**. According to Dr. Oz, many will see their muscle mass reduce by up to eight percent every ten years after age thirty, which in turn slows our metabolism. The reduction in estrogen helps the degradation of our bones. Our new fleshy arms make waving goodbye to friends a thing of the past.
- **Increased Breathlessness.** Our chest muscles begin to stiffen, and that walk across the parking lot starts to feel like a real workout.
- **Skin Loosens.** Estrogen once again leaves us hanging, literally. Skin begins to sag and lose its moisture, firmness, and elasticity. You might also find your first age spot(s) during this decade.

Weight Loss

Instead of doing the procrastination exercise sessions and starvation diets, the only thing that stands in the way is the motivation to start, to keep going, and be determined to see the end results. That's right. It's not a book, gym class, personal trainer, or even a TV show. It just starts with you. Mind over matter. When you focus, you get what you want, but the caveat is that it doesn't happen overnight. It's a process. So have fun with it. Start today with that healthy lifestyle! It only takes one step.

#OneStep

Libby's Experience: My absolute favorite fitness trend is wearables. On top of being extremely useful, they are fashionable. My advice is to invest in a Fitbit. It will motivate you to change the location of your parking spots, take the stairs more often, and find any way to increase your step count for the day.

We are all part of the sitting disease phenomena the sedentary lifestyle. I've fallen victim to the sitting disease in my IT Business Analyst position, which is known to be a desk job. Being a workaholic, I didn't realize it at first, but it didn't take long to feel soreness in my legs. After doing some research and using my expertise as a yoga instructor, I realized that my lack of movement for many hours at a time was causing immediate soreness when I stood up. I decided Fitbit was the way to go for me.

There are so many features that can help kickstart healthy lifestyle changes, such as the sleep tracker, calorie counter, and integration with other apps like MyFitnessPal, Walgreens, and Pact, just to name a few. My favorite is the challenges feature, which allows you to engage in some healthy competition with friends and family. Overall, you are supporting each other's goals for an active lifestyle. I'm always up for challenges, so hit me up at libbyfitbit@gmail.com. Yes, my Fitbit has its own email address! Sometimes I get my ten thousand steps just by marching in place watching TV! Fitbit even has special segments on celebrity fitness plans. Granted the celebrities have much more time and accountability when it comes to their fitness routine, but we can steal some of their secrets and make them our own.

Celebrity Head Shoulders Knees And Toes

Remember that old nursery rhyme "Head, shoulders, knees, toes, eyes, ears, mouth, and nose"? That's kind of how this section plays out. Starting with the head, meditation. There are so many ways that you can learn how to meditate. If you're aren't familiar with the process, meditation is bringing yourself into the present moment, taking the time to calm down and keep calm. If you are like Libby, you might want to find something to focus on instead of closing your eyes. Libby tends to fall asleep when she closes her eyes. Have a soft focus on a stationary object or even a vision board. (Sneak Preview: more on vision boards in an upcoming chapter!) Guided mediations are very helpful for finding focus. Both Oprah and Deepak Chopra have done several guided meditations that are tied to different themes such as love, happiness, and success. They are twenty-one-day programs. It supports the idea of taking twenty-one days to form a habit. Also, there are several free programs on YouTube. Just type in the word "meditation," the number of minutes, and a subject that you want to meditate on, whether it's love, prosperity, or happiness.

Next, we all love Courteney Cox's arms. She has the best arms of Hollywood stars. Here's how she gets them using the Upright Row, which targets bicep muscles and shoulders:

1. Stand with feet shoulder width apart, holding a dumbbell in each hand, palms facing the body.

2. Slowly lift dumbbells up to chest level, leading with elbows, until upper arms are level with shoulders. Return to starting position.
3. Repeat 12 to 15 times.

For the flat belly, who else better than Jillian Michaels? She makes us SHRED the weight off! We just have to pick whether it's thirty days or one week! Here's Jillian's flat belly tip:

Strengthen your core muscles. The greatest exercise you can do for your body is the plank (the standard plank and the side plank are the most popular). The plank is difficult, but it targets your core abdominal muscles, practices balance, and strengthens your chest and back muscles. The results are definitely worth it! Bye-bye, crunches!

For the toned legs: we all love the way Victoria's Secret models can walk a runway in those heels. Their secret: lunges! When you perform a lunge, you are propelling your body forward but doing a squat at the same time.

The Lunge:

1. From a standing position bring the left leg forward into a lunge, then push back to the starting position.
2. Keep your hands on your hips.
3. Repeat for a total of 5 to 10 lunges, then switch and do the right leg.
4. Rest briefly, then repeat.

The Reverse Lunge works the same muscles as the forward lunge but adds the element of balance, which requires you to engage your core as well as giving a great leg workout.

The Reverse Lunge:

1. From a standing position take your right leg back into a lunge.
2. Return to standing. Repeat, alternating legs.
3. Repeat for 2 sets of 5 to 10 reps on each leg.

The Side Lunge:

1. Start from a standing position with strong anchored feet, bring your right leg out to the side into a side lunge and squeeze. This will ensure that you engage the core. Don't go too deep with the lunge; just keep it comfortable for your level of fitness.
2. Make sure you use the ball of the foot to anchor you as you hit the floor.
3. Do 5 to 10 reps, then switch sides. Do 5 sets total.

Now put it all together by consolidating the lunge moves into a complete leg workout.

1. From a standing position, lunge forward with the right leg, return to standing, lunge to the right side and back up, then do a reverse lunge.

2. Repeat for 60 seconds, then switch to the same combination using the left leg for 60 seconds.
3. Focus on a safe, controlled movement—don't rush.

Try doing this full body workout at least once a week! You will feel sore but see results!

I Am My Own Personal Trainer

Our advice is to get a personal trainer for a month. Learn everything you can through him or her and then build your own routine. You can even get a friend to work out with you. We often exercise together when we were co-workers. It was nice to do some reps and get in some girl talk.

Rule 1: Your personal trainer is not your paid best friend!

Rule 2: Your personal trainer is not your therapist or life coach!

Rule 3: Always remember Rule 1 and Rule 2.

Libby's Experience: Here is my current plan, and I like to write it out as if a personal trainer wrote it up for me so it feels official. On the top of my calendar I added in my weight as well as measurements to track progress for the month. Always track progress by the month and not by the week; you will appreciate and get a real sense of your improvements this way.

Pick an exercise routine and stick to it for two months. My schedule looks like the one below:

- Monday: Yoga
- Tuesday: Spin
- Wednesday: Rest
- Thursday: Yoga
- Friday: Gym Time
- Saturday: Change it up to Pilates Reformer. This is the one workout that makes me cry!

- Sunday: Rest, but create your workout plan for the week. Make planning fun by using colored pens on a printed calendar.

Play Ball

Not everyone is cut out for the solo elliptical session or indoor rowing machine. The need to be in motion without the hamster wheel feeling can have you racing to the nearest field hockey . . . field. It sounds difficult to pick a sport and hop on a team, but it's surprisingly easy. There are beginner dodgeball, football, and tennis teams that can be found easily using www.meetup. com, or you can start your own. And for those who would like to remain solo, martial arts, fencing, swimming, and skiing are great picks. We're never too old to feel like we're in high school again. But don't expect to letter in adult flag football. This is a great way to find a potential date as well. Libby knows a couple that met on the soccer field!

Jillian's Experience: After living in the Sunshine State for two years, I finally decided to join a Stand Up Paddleboard class through www.meetup.com. I have no problem heading to events like this by myself, but the fear of falling held me back. Since I am not a great swimmer, I knew I would flail and flap about in the most embarrassing way, trying to save my life if I lost my balance. I don't know why, but I volunteered to be the first participant to paddle into the water. I began on my knees and slowly rose to my feet, leading the group around the intra-coastal waters. It was by far the easiest activity I had done in years, and I took a second to kick myself for not doing it earlier! In fact, I was able to kick myself and keep my balance without falling. Again, too easy. I was so sore the next day that I could barely move, but I wore it like a badge of honor.

#APPLove

Being smart phone addicts, we love fitness apps. These are our favorites, available for both iPhone and Android.

Libby's favorite fitness apps (iPhone):

- Fitbit
- Pact
- Abs Workout: Getting a Perfect Belly
- 30 Day Squat Challenge

Jillian's favorite fitness apps (Android):

- My Fitness Pal (tracks calories, water intake, and much more)
- Samsung Galaxy Fitness (tracks number of steps, walking, 5k training, etc.)
- YouTube Fitness Blender

The best part is that all of these apps are free! It's like having your own personal trainer with you 24/7. Once you stick to a workout plan, the habit is formed, and you'll automatically want to get your workout in.

#WorkOutFashion

Can you wear your nightwear to work? Can you get comfortable sleep in your work clothes? The answer is most likely no, unless you work from home in your pajamas. If so, you have our dream job!

So what makes your workout clothes any different? Sure, you can wear that baggy shirt and straight-legged yoga pants, but can you see your results? Not really. Where is all your hard work hiding? Don't get, me wrong, I, Libby, go to a group class at times and look at the mirror and see my bloated belly or flabby arms. I feel bad for a second before I move on to how great my red lipstick (yes, put on your red lipstick) looks and how fun the class is, and slowly those insecurities go away. Finally, one month into the workout plan, I can start seeing that the outfit is not as tight as it was before. I feel more confident in the way I look, all the while singing "Shake It Off." Got to love Taylor!

Sit Up Straight

Bad posture does not match the newfound confidence and poise we exude in our thirties (use British charm school teacher accent when reading). Do you know where this bad habit is likely coming from? That does not mean we were all sitting like ballerinas before we started carrying mini flat screens in our purses, but they're definitely having a surprising effect. It's called ihunch/text neck. The two to four hours we spend hunched over our phones each day puts pressure on our spine. The more you channel Lurch from the Addams family, the more you increase the pressure. The end result could be surgery to fix the degeneration that arises, but there are less severe symptoms that can make your day-to-day life a complete pain in the neck (pun intended). Headaches, constipation, depression, and chronic pain are linked to bad posture. Plus, you miss out on the boost in serotonin that is associated with good posture. Lift your phone closer to eye level to reduce the strain when you LOL.

Health Concerns And Family History

Our twenties were filled with thoughts of invincibility (and double cheeseburgers). When it was time to choose health insurance during annual enrollment, we were more concerned with getting the plan that put only the slightest dent in our paychecks. Now, before we reach for the cheapest plan, we at least consider the ones that could take better care of us as we age. It's a gradual shift that acknowledges the fact that we're getting older and may need to reduce our risks and our deductibles.

We need to pay attention to the illnesses that run in our families and get wind of them as our loved ones they age along with us. Below are some of the ailments we need to watch for, delay, and avoid:

- Hormone Changes
- High Blood Pressure
- Breast Health
- Diabetes

- Eye Diseases
- The C-Word (Cancer)

Let's Hear It For The Babes

If you're like us, you plan to have little ones during this decade. It's pretty exciting to think about chasing after your toddler and teaching your tiny miracle the ways of the world. Here's the kicker: do you envision yourself running out of breath mid-chase, or are you fit and ready for this new chapter of your life? For many, our early thirties are the best time for childrearing because we have more money, a better sense of self, and are likely still holding onto the remains of our stamina. It's paramount that we find a fitness routine that we can continue before, during, and after pregnancy. Also, a healthy body weight is key to increasing your odds of a healthy pregnancy and fewer complications. According to Lauren Gelman of www.Parents.com, a body mass index (BMI) between nineteen and twenty-four is ideal for getting pregnant and a safer delivery.

Smiley Face

According to the Oxford Dictionary, the word of the year 2015 was not a word at all, but rather the crying-with-joy emoji we all know and love. When we get text messages with emojis, they always make me smile. Studies show that each time you smile you are throwing a little feel-good party in your brain. You can look at yourself in the mirror and over-analyze or just look at yourself and smile. See the difference. It's been scientifically proven that smiling will help out regardless of the situation. Our absolute favorite quote by an unknown author is "Keep a smile on your face, because you never know who is falling in love with that smile."

Full Length

Staying active is obviously an important step in maintaining your health. We all have a picture of health in our mind and the drive to reach it. But during the process of moving toward the ideal, we may forget to feel great about where we are now. We learn to pinch, prod, and mentally punish ourselves for having too little or extra weight. Women are constantly being shown images geared toward promoting these negative feelings. But it's key to understand that you can love where you are and still want to improve. In fact, accepting your current self can propel you to take care of your body in a more loving way and make exercise feel like the next best step. So, yes, go ahead, proudly wave to your friend while wearing your sleeveless shirt. And tomorrow, we work.

LESSONS LEARNED IN OUR 30S:

1. Mind over matter.
2. Count your steps.
3. Exercise one day, rest one day.
4. Dress the part.
5. Smile.

#ChowTime

#Foodie

We both love to eat! The fancier our meals, the more pictures we take and post online. We love trying new restaurants. With that said, we do make it a point to eat healthily on a regular basis. We're sure you've noticed that one of the most sought-after habits is to eat healthier foods. But sometimes (all the time) that apple tastes much better inside of a pie. As we get a little older, rounder, and slower, we need to take more responsibility of how and what we eat to ensure long, healthy lives.

Jillian's Favorites: Ethiopian food and sushi.

Libby's Favorites: Beef Fajitas and Thai Red Curry (not together, though)

Healthy Eating Habits

Abs are made in the kitchen. Depending on who you ask, making the decision to exercise is easy compared to the hourly task of choosing the best foods. We are constantly tempted to grab chips, candy bars, and pizza. There are times where we win and feel great that our self-control is in check. Other times, Domino's is victorious. And who would want to give up milk chocolate for life? That would be a real tragedy. Listen to your body, and do the best you can at every meal. In today's "grab-n-go" world, it's too easy to ignore our health and not be mindful of what we put in our bodies. How often have we walked into a McDonald's to buy a double cheeseburger, fries, and a soda for lunch and dinner just because it was across the street from the office, and we were in a time crunch? Don't get us wrong: we can all have cake and eat it, too—just not for every meal. Plus, eating healthy can be so confusing. Fat is bad—no, wait, it's good. Snacking should be avoided—but you should eat several mini-meals each day. There are just too many ever-changing rules to keep up with. Don't worry, we've got you covered. Keep reading.

Food Is Medicine

You may have heard the saying, "There's a reason the word 'die' is in diet," but eating healthier doesn't necessarily mean giving up your favorite fast foods and immediately becoming a vegetarian. Eating healthier means gradually eating less of what may be unhealthy and replacing it with foods of higher nutritional value.

We don't normally think about how bananas improve immunity or how pears contain twenty-four percent of our daily fiber needs. Often times we just eat what we like. The fact that spinach fights acne isn't at the forefront of our minds. But what if it were? We know that fruits and veggies are great for our health, but what if we remembered that each bite was delicious medicine strengthening our bodies. Would you still want that cheeseburger? Probably. But would you eat it? Maybe not. Changing the way you eat in your thirties will transform your life. A plant-based, fiber-filled diet will create a healthy gut by producing healthy bacteria. Lean meat is good, but less is best.

Learning to eat better doesn't have to be painful. Whether you want to lose weight, detoxify your body, or simply just want to improve your eating habits, here are some tips to help you make some healthier choices when it comes to your grocery shopping, meals, and snacks.

Less Is More

When you use smaller plates, you eat less food. According to the Small Plate Movement, you can lose eighteen pounds in a year by using plates that are between nine and ten inches in diameter. We wonder how the French are able to eat rich foods and still live healthier, longer lives. The secret is in the portion and rate of speed when eating. Most of us eat too fast and therefore consume more calories before our bodies let us know that we're actually full. Eating at a slower rate will allow your body to catch up and tell you when you're full. And those smaller portions give you the opportunity to savor your food as an added bonus.

Foodie Shop

By going to the farmers' market, you're guaranteed to get the freshest in-season produce available, and the produce is—wait for it—locally sourced! Additionally, it's a great way to connect with merchants and the farmers themselves and learn more about what you're bringing home. And maybe even find a potential date.

If you do go to the grocery store, shop around the perimeter. Grocery stores place their clean, natural, and perishable items around their stores, with all the packaged stuff in between. These perimeter items include fruits, vegetables, dairy, meat, and seafood. So the next time you stop at Kroger, you'll want to focus on what's on the outside rather than the center aisles

Jillian's Experience: I have a love/hate relationship with shopping for food. I love reading labels and spotting that weird vegetable that I've never seen before. But I'm not a fan of preparing a list, and the anticipation of shopping seems like an ordeal every time I need food. Once I have that strange veggie in my basket, I never know what to purchase next and end up wandering around without a plan. Or, I get ambitious and buy two weeks' worth of food that I should probably just throw away once I get home instead of fourteen days later. To get a handle on the grocery game, I scoured the Web and found a great way to reduce the wander and shop smarter:

Take a page out of The Everygirl.com Grocery List

- 2 Proteins (one must be a fish)
- 2 Veggies
- 2 fruits
- Eggs
- 1 Cheese
- 1 Grain (quinoa/brown rice)

Purchase smart snacks for the week like nuts and dark chocolate

Add More Veggies To Your Plate Or Blender

Libby's Experience: Remember when your parents always told you to eat your vegetables? That's exactly what my parents told me every day, especially at snack time: eat your veggies, or you won't grow! I'm not sure how much of that's really true, but I do I wish I would have kept up with my parents' eating habits. They grew their own vegetables and ate every single one of them. I called this the Backyard Diet.

The Harvard School of Public Health recommends adults on a 2000-calorie diet consume 2 ½ cups of vegetables each day. Two of these cups should consist of raw leafy green vegetables like spinach, kale, or romaine lettuce. Throwing them into salads, slaws, sandwiches, and wraps is a no-brainer. You can even eat them on their own with healthy spreads like hummus. If eating crunchy greens is not your thing, you can put your serving in a blender with a ripe banana as a natural sweeteners and mix it up for a healthy and tasty smoothie. Greens are full of fiber, essential minerals, vitamins, and antioxidants that may lower your risk of heart disease, cancer, and eye disorder.

Low Inflammation Diet

Jillian's Experience: One of the biggest lessons I learned shortly after turning thirty was about a silent offender that slowly degrades your organs. It is working against you every time you eat the wrong foods. It is called inflammation. If you injure your ankle, you can see it become inflamed and swell up. Well, there are certain types of food that can cause internal inflammation you cannot see, which sets you up for diseases like dementia and diabetes down the road. Gluten, dairy, corn, soy, and nightshades are some of the foods that can mess up your gut, which is where much of your immune system lies. And it could be the reason we thirty-somethings have a hard time getting rid of our belly fat. So if our insides are constantly "on fire" and our immune system is compromised, the anti-inflammatory diet is one of the best answers. The weight gain, low energy, and high cholesterol you may be experiencing can be tamed by avoiding inflammatory foods. If you're not eating to your benefit, you're probably eating to your detriment. Stay the course and make a habit of choosing wisely.

Bad Fat To Good Fat

Within the last ten years, foods we thought were bad for us have gotten a new lease on life. The fat, cholesterol and sugar present in these foods are not responsible for heart attacks and diseases as once advertised. Live Strong has put together a great list of common foods that we can feel better about eating.

- Eggs
- Frozen Vegetables

- Avocados
- Nuts
- Shrimp
- Peanut Butter
- Potatoes
- Popcorn

No Sugar Munchies

Ease out added sugars and starches by selecting healthier alternatives. Even making one small change in a meal or snack choice can work wonders. If you prefer your sandwiches with white bread or find yourself reaching for the office candy bowl during a break at work, try making a lettuce wrap instead or getting a more natural sugar fix by topping Greek yogurt with your favorite berries. Swap out white rice for brown rice. J.J Virgin, author of the bestselling The Sugar Impact Diet, details the hidden sugars in the foods we eat, such as dried fruits and salad dressing. She encourages you to move from the high- to low-sugar foods to prevent the long- and short-term side effects of a life with sugar.

Go Nuts Over Nut Based Milk

Speaking of healthier alternatives, replacing cow's milk with nut-based milk (almond, cashew, macadamia, and hazelnut are some popular ones) can add some more vitamins and minerals to your diet, such as potassium and vitamin E. Additionally, they're generally lower in saturated fat and cholesterol. You'll want to make sure they are fortified with calcium and vitamin D, though, as not all nut-based milks are created equal. But they're pretty versatile: pour them into your cereal, blend them into shakes, and mix them in your morning coffee.

Come To Me Food

As we mentioned before, part of the reason eating healthy can be difficult is because we live in a "grab-n-go" world. Sometimes we just need to lessen the time it takes to research and shop around for healthy food. Luckily, thanks to continued innovation and the Internet, there are services out there to help us choose and better prepare our meals.

Have limits on your time in the kitchen? You can now have curated healthy meals delivered to your door. You can choose whether you want breakfast, lunch, or dinner, and select a preset plan to get X number of chef-prepared meals delivered to you weekly. The service offers programs based on your personal goals, like weight loss, lowering your cholesterol, or building endurance for working out.

#MealPrep

Meal Planning is not just for the organized or those who bring their dinner leftovers into work. It's a great time and money saver and prevents us from stressing over our meals and finding excuses to binge on junk. Think of it as a uniform for your diet. Instead of spending money, minutes, and gas at a drive-thru or restaurant, you get to whip out a quick healthy meal for lunch. You might even get to make new friends in the break room or convert your current lunch friends into believers. You'll need the following:

- The information from above on where and how to get healthier foods.
- Meal containers for each meal of the day (except maybe dinner) plus snacks.
- Two hours for prep
- Pinterest

The best day to start is on a Sunday, if that's the beginning of your week. Take two hours to cook and build your meals, and then celebrate because you're winning the war on food. Your meals don't have to be boring, but this process and consistency could have you missing your old ways of eating out "restaurant style." Feel free to switch your breakfast for lunch and make two or three different types of snacks during the week if you need some "excitement" with your meals. We won't lie: we miss those days in our twenties when going out for lunch daily with our crew was the thing to do. But the physical and mental results from planning meals and knowing exactly what's in our food keep us on the path to being lean and mean (only because "lean" and "happy" don't rhyme).

What Would You Like To Drink?

Let's Meet Over Coffee

Libby's Experience: I always tell my friends that coffee should be running through an IV line for me. I also love fun coffee mugs; think about it … an accessory to your coffee. I can use an elegant, trendy, or just plain funny mug, and it automatically uplifts my spirits at the office. One of my favorites is an anatomy mug that I got from Etsy because it helps me with teaching yoga. Back to the truth of the matter: coffee is good for you! Recent studies in 2015 show that coffee is actually a lifesaver. People who drink regular, moderate amounts of coffee are less likely to die from a range of diseases, from diabetes to heart disease. The cutoff seems to be around five cups a day and even decaf coffee helps, the team at Harvard University's school of public health found. "The main message is that regular consumption, meaning three to five cups of coffee a day, is associated with lower risk in total mortality and mortality from several causes like diabetes, cardiovascular disease and suicide," Frank Hu, a professor of nutrition and epidemiology who helped lead the study, told NBC News. Maybe we will have a whole section on Coffee IV lines in Lessons in Our (Early) 40s!

TeaTime

After water, tea is the world's most widely consumed drink. And although it's rich in history and tradition, tea is really very simple. Here are some types of pure teas: white, green, oolong, and black. Tea connoisseurs will not have milk with their tea—they have it plain (no Chai Tea Latte from Starbucks). However, there are plenty of black teas for a classic flavor that are enjoyable with a splash or milk or a cube of sugar added, and there are many traditions of adding milk, sugar, or both to tea. Finally, in the South we love our (lightly sweetened) Sweet Tea!

#Cheers

Let's clink our glasses in favor of champagne. It's not just for celebrations, but for good health. Thanks to polyphenols (antioxidants), a glass once a week will lower your blood pressure, which in turn reduces your chances of heart attack and stroke. These are not immediate concerns, as we are in our thirties but it can improve short term memory over time. This could reduce the amount of time spent looking for your misplaced cell phone (did you check under the blanket?). Also, it beats out both red and white wine at just ninety calories per serving.

PopTime –Do You Have Pop?

Libby's Experience: A coworker from the Northeast once asked me about pop, and I asked, "Why do you need my dad?" I shortly realized this was slang for Coke or soda. I wasn't a big fan of soda until recently, and then I got hooked on Coca-Cola and not the Diet or the Zero versions; the real stuff can be addictive. According Sara Bleich, an associate professor in the department of health policy and management at Johns Hopkins, you have to walk five miles to burn off the 250 calories in a twenty-ounce can. And don't forget there are about ten teaspoons of liquid sugar each one. It is not good for you! I try to make a pact with myself to only use soda as a reward instead of a daily fix.

#JustAddWater –Staying Hydrated Keeps Us Healthy
The body of an adult human, on average, contains sixty percent water. Most of the water in the human body is contained inside our billions of cells.. Water helps the kidneys function, increases our energy and hydrates our skin among other benefits. Most of us are dehydrated without even realizing it; so grab another glass of the good stuff before you head to the next chapter.

LESSONS LEARNED IN OUR 30S:

1. Start Your Day with Breakfast. Breakfast jump-starts your metabolism
2. Limit Fast Food. Plan your meals. It saves money and time.
3. Eat More Veggies. Uses the Pact app to keep track of veggies, but beware if you miss: you might be paying the app $5!
4. Hydrate with Water. You need water to survive.

5. Don't Skip Meals. Skipping meals slows down your metabolism and causes you to be starving later on, which can ultimately lead to overdoing it or making poor choices.
6. Avoid the Soda. Forgoing soda helps with cutting out sugar and unnecessary calories.

#StyleMe

FashionFinds —"I Have Nothing To Wear"

Dressing the part is a great way to beef up your confidence, and boost your personal brand. It's the first thing everyone sees when you step into a room and draws people and experiences to you. We still care what some people think. We like to present ourselves in the best light and will silently judge anyone else using that same metric. But since we don't get too carried away with the judgement of others in this decade, we don't want that to work against us by avoiding the rules of the polished.

Sometimes we underestimate the feelings that arise from looking good. We've been doing the whole clothes-buying thing for a while now, and it tends to have a "the struggle is real" feeling when it doesn't have to. In fact, it shouldn't. Eliminate that struggle so you can step out feeling great at least ninety percent of the time. I know we're going to have our bad days and reach for the college sweatshirt and the leggings with the holes. And I'm not talking about the holes you put your legs through. Plus, we are expected to look that much more stylish and respectable whether we're in a traditional office setting or blogging away at our local Starbucks. We tend to feel great in things that feel good on us and need to show off our eight-plus years of experience in getting dressed as a full-fledged adult. Put that on your resume. No . . . don't.

Women spend an average of sixteen minutes deciding what to wear on weekday mornings and thirty minutes on Saturdays and Sundays. Karen Pine, a professor in the School of Psychology at University of Hertfordshire interviewed, one hundred women and found that 73% shopped for clothes at least every few months." The majority of women, or 96%, "believed that what they wear affects how confident they feel."

What you wear has a direct impact on how you feel about yourself. Your clothes reveal a lot about who you are as a person. Below is an in-depth chart on the psychology of your behavior with regards to clothing:

Situation	Analysis	Final Answer
Never throw away or donate any of your clothes.	Hoarder	Take out all items that are too big, small, ripped, torn, or outdated.
Wear only neutrals.	Invisible	Add pop of color through either accessorizing or the outfit itself.
Dress in clothing too large for your body.	Body Image	Shop with a true friend or personal shopper to find out what looks great on you, ignore sizes, and get used to wearing clothes that really fit your body.
Have been told you dress inappropriately or too sexy.	Attention Seeker	Choose outfits based on those around you, thinking about the image you want in given situations.
Dress too young (or too old) for your age.	Not Living in the Present	Dress for your achievements, such as new job or first dates, rather a specific age group.
Are always in work clothes.	Workaholic	Have fun with your wardrobe.
Are covered in designer logos.	Name Dropper	Practice the "Hi Lo method." Wear Target with Prada! Mix it up!

#Purging

Jillian's Experience: Before we discuss the things you should have in your new era of adulti-ness, we should tell you what to throw away. I like to use the "KonMari method" of getting my closet together. Libby found this method when she went down the Internet rabbit hole several months ago. Marie Kondo is a bestselling, organization guru based in Japan.

Her method is to pull everything out of your closet and hold up each item one by one. Ask yourself if it brings you joy. If the answer is no, you know what to do. This could take a while; give yourself some time, so you don't get overwhelmed by all of the clothing you've accumulated over the last several years. While you have everything lying all over your bedroom or closet floor, determine which items just need some polishing up to make it back into the rotation.

Method 2 Madness

There is a method to the madness. Never worry about picking your outfit again! Unfortunately, we don't have that luxurious Clueless closet system; but we are extremely thankful for the invention of the full-length mirror. It's like having a fashion show every time we choose an outfit to wear.

Libby's Experience: With my job, I travel often, and sometimes it's for two weeks straight with no breaks to come home. I always panic at the idea of packing for long trips. You just never know when the perfect outfit is left at home. I tried out this "capsule wardrobe" idea that I saw on Pinterest. It makes life much easier, and I never waste time on my impromptu fashion shows of what to wear for work or traveling for fun anymore.

Now, what to wear for a date is more complicated. Dating is complicated overall. That's why we have a whole chapter on it! Most importantly, every single item hanging in my closet is something I would love to wear at any time, and when I'm done, it is donated for someone else to love.

Capsule Wardrobe

First, choose a limited color palette: two to four colors should be enough. Libby's favorites are black, white, navy blue, and green. Jillian's favorites are grey, white, pink, and purple.

Next, select the following items based on your color palette:

- 6 shirts
- 5 bottoms
- 2 jackets
- 2 dresses
- 2 bags
- 6 pairs of shoes

Every bottom needs to match three different tops. Following these rules, you should have almost thirty outfits.

Tailor Made

Many of the items above may already be in your closet, but you might need to go shopping (if they don't fit well) or visit a tailor. Does anybody know a good tailor? That's the question you should be asking your friends and those you see in well-fitting clothing. A great tailor can make you look like you stepped out of a magazine. In our twenties, this was something we thought about doing. But in our thirties, it's something we need to do in order to get it to-ge-ther (snaps fingers!). It's basically an investment in yourself that will pay dividends. The tailored look says, "I care how I present myself."

Jillian's Experience: If you're like me, you arrive at work on Monday looking a lot sharper than on Thursday. My level of caring about what I wear for work takes a dip after Tuesday and doesn't recover until I've had a few days off. That means I bring out the oversized sweater or the button-down with the gap in the boob area when I know I shouldn't, but it's all I have on such short notice. Who knew I had to go to work five consecutive days in a row? Having everything in your closet fit just right means there are no more days like this! You can pull anything from your closet with the same indifference on Thursday and have it fit like it's Monday. Bonus: you can wear a size medium and have the tailor transform that extra-large dress you bought on clearance.

Next understand which style is preferred for your body type. For example, if you're top heavy, wrap dresses and three-quarter-sleeve shirts won't let you down, but evil spaghetti straps have it in for you. If you're a pear shape, you need A-line skirts and flat-front trousers more than pencil skirts. When we wear the clothing that fits our shape instead of what looks good on a hanger—or a model who is so not our size—we set ourselves up for failure. We don't have room in our budgets, closets, or schedules for a bunch of no-gos.

Finally, get a personal stylist. It seems like a magical, frivolous experience for those with time and money. But if you think about the time spent putting together outfits on your own—and not succeeding—or the money spent on items that go with nothing in your closet, you'll make out better with some assistance. If you would rather not shop for your body type and just buy cute stuff when you see it, let the personal shopper see it instead. He or she can hook you up and have you on your way, within your budget. Jillian's sister prefers the personal shoppers at Nordstrom, while her coworker prefers the online version at Stich Fix. It's efficient, fun, and kind of exciting to let them handle your wardrobe needs. Remember to stick to your color palette!

Looking Polished

Lazy girl's tip for looking polished: rely on the blazer to get you through any challenging outfit days. Not to mention that jeans and t-shirts get a boost of style when paired with a blazer. It rounds out most looks and makes you appear to be an authority on . . . everything. It's stylish, and you look like you tried and succeeded. The best colors to start with are black, white, and navy since they're great neutrals. After that you can graduate to one with a pop of color. If you are already hip to blazers and have a few, it's time to get that hot pink one you were afraid to buy.

Jillian's Experience: Comfortable shoes are a must! It's time to purchase those higher-end, higher quality shoes; you deserve them! In my twenties, you would never catch me in flats. If you didn't see me in heels that day, it was because I wasn't at work. Unfortunately, they were not the best quality of shoes. Now, I come up with four different excuses for why I need to be in my Tory Burch flats at any given moment. They don't usually project that glamorous, sexy look but we still need to wear what makes us feel good physically. Mix up your style with wedges and shorter heels. My favorite high heels are from Stuart Weitzman, and I can walk ten thousand steps before I curse his name. That's pretty impressive as far as I'm concerned. The message here: don't give up on heels. They won't give up on you.

#Accessorize Me

Let's complete your new look. These are our suggestions for accessories:

- Necklaces. Classic pearl or diamond (or CZ) pedant, statement necklace
- Earrings. Diamond stud, CZ stud, hoops, chandelier earrings, simple drop earrings.
- Rings. Simple design, stackable rings, as well as cocktail designs
- Bracelets. Statement bracelets, yogi-beaded bracelet, thin stackable bracelets.
- Bags. Elegant clutch, iconic bag, work bag.

More Tips For A Polished Look

The foundation of looking polished is composed of the hardest working, but unseen, items of clothing. They hold everything together, so the rest of you can shine bright like a diamond. If you haven't guessed it by now, it's your underwear and shapewear. We already learned in our mid-to-late twenties that these items are important to get right and that statistics say we're always wearing the wrong size. Well, how about now? You've probably gained a bit of weight and are due for a trip to the lingerie section. You're going through the same fitting issues of yesteryear and need to take a minute to figure out the new, slightly larger you. While we know you're planning to lose that extra seven pounds, just go ahead and get a few items that match your current size. Let the underwear and shapewear smooth out some of those bulges and awkward spots that are keeping you from looking like an "It Girl." Even a woman who wears a size two can have some unflattering spots! Grab some Spanx and your new, well-fitting bra and head to a mirror to see the transformation. It really is a transformation, so don't sleep on this!

Also, try getting your "nails did" on a regular basis. Polished nails can give you a jolt of confidence and leave a better impression. Bare nails can leave you feeling a little undone so make sure that they're well groomed. Chipped polish should be rectified A.S.A.P. because it gives off the message of not taking pride in yourself. Don't forget the toes! You'll think better of yourself if you don't skip them, and you definitely can't grab for those sandals at a moment's notice.

Signature Scent

Next, find your signature scent. We all know that mature lady who floats by, releasing a wonderful cloud of smell-good that awakens your senses. It smells mature and clean but slightly spicy and floral. Yep, it smells like someone who is successful at being an adult. While you breathe deeply for the next thirty seconds, you wonder what she's wearing and if you'll ever smell that great. Your fun and fruity Bath and Body Works scent smells good, but you also know that you've been wearing it since 2009. It's time to upgrade to a potion that a twenty-something would not reach for then wear it like you own it. Because you do, since you probably bought it. Jillian's favorite scent is Not a Perfume by Juliette Has A Gun and Libby loves Hermès Elixir des Merveilles.

Steam Me

Jillian's Experience: Lastly, buy a clothing steamer. This saves me, so much time in the morning! I don't have to unfold an ironing board and wait for some undetermined amount of time for it to heat up. Truthfully, I haven't ironed in years, so any iron advancements have been lost on me. I have a steamer that takes one minute or less to heat up and produce enough steam to knock wrinkles out of almost anything. I then move onto the next clothing item with a quickness that can't even be compared to using an iron. And if it's something I've already worn that's getting an encore before heading to the dry cleaners, the steamer refreshes it. So yeah, I'm on Team Steam all the way.

We want your early thirties to be a time where the closet conundrums are smoothed out and dressing is more seamless, enjoyable, and less time consuming. We are sending a message to the outside world that we are poised, confident, and polished. The world is then more likely to take us seriously and push us out in front to reap the benefits. This includes better dating partners, job opportunities, and even friends. If you have great clothes, you'll wear great clothes, even on your way to the store to buy milk. And you never know who you'll run into along the way!

LESSONS LEARNED IN OUR 30S

1. Pick Your Color Palette
2. If You Haven't Worn It in Twelve Months, Donate It.
3. Stay Classy on the Accessories
4. Get Steamy

#MoneyMagic

ere is a cool, weird trick to make a million dollars in less than a week: become Walter White of Breaking Bad. For the rest of us, we'll need to continue with legal ways to become financially free. Money makes our lives go 'round, and acquiring it can keep us pretty busy. Unfortunately, so can spending. It's a topic that is boring and exciting at the same time and requires more willpower than skill. Since we've overcome our fair share of mountains and molehills in the financial arena, we can tell you what we've learned and wished we would have done more of along the way. So let's get to it!

You're at the point where you're making more money than ever before. The roommate situation is kaput because you think you're too mature. And you like wine now. Yes, you've stepped out of the era of blowing dollars on clubs and rounds of shots, but you've replaced it with higher rent and pinot. While these are normal wants, instead try moving more money into your Roth IRA, investment accounts, and emergency funds. In your twenties you probably saved some of your paychecks—maybe not an impressive amount, but a sum that seemed cool at the time. Now you're in your thirties and things just . . . got . . . real. It's like someone walked over and told you that this whole "work" thing will last for thirty-five more years. Let's take a minute to tweak our money mindset and how we stash the cash.

Money Magic: Money Mindset

Money Is Your Friend

We want you to take stock of how you're feeling as you read through this chapter. Do you feel fearful or empowered and excited? We know saving is more challenging because of our mind-sets and our need for Venti Mocha Lattes. But think back to a time when you had the most money in your account or saw your investments growing. How did that feel? It probably felt like satisfaction, happiness, security, and accomplishment. It's better to feel great about accumulating money than spending it. That's mentality you should work toward.

It shouldn't be used as an excuse for why you can't fulfill your dreams or the source of complaints about your life. Part of what separates the wealthy from the not-so-wealthy is their attitude about money. Those habitual thoughts of not having enough or how hard it is to obtain will not only send a message of lack into the universe, but will make you uninspired to take action to bring more money into your life.

The best way to break yourself of these beliefs is to first recognize that a belief is just a repetitive thought. Then create statements like "Money is fun to have and comes quickly and easily," or "I am happy I have what I need to pay this bill." Since beliefs are repetitive thoughts, you'll have to decide how long you'll need to work to create a new mind-set. While saying these statements, you need to generate the best feeling you can reach for to make this real. This will open you up to feeling comfortable about money and knowing that more of it is attainable. Feelings are what we're trying to change. And in turn, those feelings will change your actions.

Write down on a piece of paper how much money you want right now. Every day write down that exact same amount. We want you to know exactly what that amount feels like. Once you get this habit going, you'll slowly see money trickling in (See Bonus Chapter Ask, Believe Receive).

Money Magic: Where Is Your Stash?

Are you interested in working your current job for thirty more years? Even if you are, should it be an option or an obligation? There is a small, growing movement of young people opting out of the forty-hour work week in favor of financial independence and early retirement. It starts by saving a percentage of your paycheck each period and putting it in a place to grow. We know this seems like the same motions you make anyway, but the portion of your paycheck in these accounts should be at least forty percent, and the time frame is usually ten to fifteen years.

Me: I Want To Buy New Shoes!
Bank Account: Please Don't!

The more common percentages for saving and spending are 50-30-20. This means 50 percent of your earnings go to bills, 30 percent is for fun, and you save 20 percent. Why should your road to financial freedom rely on just 20 percent of your income? Take at least 10 percent from fun and reduce your bills by 10 percent. Try any combination that bumps up your savings category. The goal here is to accumulate enough money and work only if and/or when you feel like it. This flies in the face of conventional timetables, but it bears asking, who made this "retire when the government says you can" method anyway?

Jillian's Experience: Here's how I do it. I work in a corporate setting and receive a paycheck twice a month, and as soon as the funds hit my account, I decide on the dollar amount I to happily set aside. As a personal rule, I must set aside at least 30 percent. Along with fun money, I will leave the money needed for fixed and fixed-variable expenses (e.g., food) in my checking account. I know that funds set aside for some arbitrary point in the future still doesn't activate that sense of urgency in our thirties, but the importance of it all starts to grow.

Libby's Experience: My parents taught me the importance of saving money. They are subject matter experts in this field. Unfortunately, I don't do it as much as I should because I have a shopping problem! However, the more you can save, the better it is. You really don't need every color of David Yurman bracelets. One statement piece is more valuable than ten. I am finally beginning to practice this mentality. As Jillian mentioned above, you should save about 30 percent of your income; some people save more, some people save less. Based on my experience, any amount on every single paycheck, whether it's $100 or $1,400, will all add up at the end. Just don't give up. If you can only save a little in the beginning, that is better than nothing. My suggestion is to do an automatic transfer every week.

Make Saving Automatic

This is for both Lazy McLazyson and the diligent saver. In your banking and investment accounts, choose the automatic transfer option to have funds transferred from your checking account, where it's easy to get lost on a new pair of shoes. You'll be surprised at how much money you are able to put away and how you didn't even miss it. When you look back on this day and see how far you've come, it'll all be worth it.

How Is Your Emergency Fund Doing?

Do you have enough saved for that new (hopefully pre-owned) car or transmission? There are some emergencies that are bound to happen, ranging from car repairs to medical expenses. Are you ready for them? If not, you are missing out on some peace of mind. Depending on who you ask, your emergency funds should cover three to nine months of living expenses. Start saving for this first if you haven't already. We're in our thirties, so we've already had at least one money emergency happen by now. At the very least, let this be a reminder to replenish. So start right now. Literally—right now. Go to your bank app and transfer what you can to your emergency savings account. Go ahead. We'll wait.

Invest In The Market

By now you should have some funds invested in the stock market, and your 401k should be rocking and rolling. If this is not the case, you'll be playing catch-up for a bit. While your 401k may not completely set you free at re-tirement, it's a big plus to have in your investment arse-nal. Take advantage of the free money from the employer match, and increase your contributions from your own salary to reduce your taxable income if that will benefit you. When you receive your annual raise, increase your

401k contributions by one percent And while you're at it, give your 401k financial adviser a call to make sure your portfolio is still a winner..

Most of us are not investment savvy and will likely need some set-it-and-forget-it options. You don't have to go very deep into Google before Vanguard and other low-fee index funds pop up. These funds have multiple stocks and other vehicles bundled together to form an index. In addition to this benefit, the fees are very low, and that will save you thousands of dollars in the long run. Plus, Warren Buffet is a fan of this type of passive investing, so it must hold some weight! These funds should be in both your 401k and your taxable investment accounts. Remember, it is important to have products in your portfolio that do not require you to turn fifty-nine and a half or sixty-five years old. Any dreams of retiring early (or at all!) are likely dependent on this fact, and you'll need a lump sum (and a strategy) to accomplish this. As always, contact your tax and investment professional for more information.

With all of this investing action, don't forget about your Roth IRA. This will not get you to the Promised Land in thirty years, but it will be yet another great place to stash cash. This individual retirement savings account has the benefit of tax-free withdrawals and lets you invest your money almost anywhere including money markets, exchange traded funds and traditional savings accounts. Check the contribution limits each year to make sure you don't exceed them.

And while it has not been made fact, rumors of the decline of Social Security for our generation have been circulating for years. Millennials have been encouraged to establish our own path to self-sufficiency without depending solely on the government to provide in our old age. There have been too many hands in the pot and not enough contributors to cover the outflows. At this time, we can likely count on limited assistance, which means we are unsure of the impact it will have on our lives and our retirement calculator. With no guarantees ahead, it's better to exclude this from our expectations and focus on empowering ourselves to slowly build our own nest egg.

Retirement savings gender gap describes why women need to save more for the reasons below:

- Women are expected to live an average of three years longer than men.
- Earn less than our male counterparts.
- Will exit the workplace for an average of eleven years to raise children/care for elders.

Money Magic: So Where Do You Go Shopping?

In our twenties, we focused on getting low-quality, cheap but acceptable things we could buy at our local Scandinavian marketplace. With this strategy, the quality can be an afterthought, and you easily fall out of love with your items. And where are those things now? Probably in your closet, den, and bedroom, making you feel like a kid. Or maybe you sold them on Craigslist and haven't replaced them. Your home is your sanctuary, and it should feel that way. Your closet should be filled with items that help you present yourself as a capable, professional adult. Your kitchen should have proper knives.

Planning and spending in categories that create peace of mind, pride in your home, and confidence in self are great at this age. Look at services that could free up your time, such as having groceries delivered and cleaning services, to maximize your time spent on growing your passion and clearing your mind of clutter. The point we're trying to make here is that you should make your surroundings and your lifestyle a priority.

We call this calculated spending. Spend on items that meaningful and are considered quality. And remember, none of this has to be expensive. So, yes, spending is okay to a certain extent. But some of us can justify all spending and claim it's in the name of quality and peace of mind when it really isn't. We won't point any fingers, but we will give you some pointers.

Employ the forty-eight-hour rule. Don't buy the item or service as soon as you know it exists. Wait two days and then figure out if you really want it or if it's just an impulse buy. Libby usually buys things she dreams about three times. You'll feel empowered at how you resisted temptation or excited that the item or service really added value to your life.

Libby's Experience: Budgeting yourself for cash-only weeks will help you manage your necessary and unnecessary spending. In my twenties, I never thought of money this way. I had a YSL umbrella. I had an apartment that was very chic. I never shopped sales. I just bought whatever I wanted whenever I wanted. In my thirties, I have an even better apartment and very nice furniture; however, I bought them all on sale. Now I never buy anything full price because I truly believe everything goes on sale eventually. They can't trick me anymore.

It's a tough lesson, but you will appreciate your financial security, your lifestyle, and most importantly, your happiness. As you're drinking that pinot noir, don't worry about the second glass. You deserve it. You saved the money, so reward yourself.

Money Magic: More Money

How many of y'all wake up in the morning and just think, I want to be rich!" You're in luck; we think it, too, which is why we felt that the financial chapter is so important (and the longest!). In our thirties we think more about investments and long-term benefits. We also become inspired by our environment and begin thinking of ways to make more money. With all of the twenty-somethings creating startups from simple ideas and turning them into billions, the question "Why didn't I think of that?" is on repeat in our minds. Should we have just become superstar programmers in Silicon Valley or Wall Street investment bankers? Probably. Yes. But there's still an abundance of money to be made where you are.

#SideHustle

So you like to blog? How can you turn that into dollars? Are you into dividend-paying stocks? Aim to have at least two income streams in the next six to twelve months. If you're scared to take a leap because of the risks, think about it this way: you're taking a bigger risk by having just one income stream. If you need help finding a few, try searching Pinterest to lead you to the ideas of those who have successfully made extra money. If you get really good at it, you may even want to quit your day job.

With everything you do, the best question to ask yourself first is, "Am I adding value to the lives of others?" Don't put the cart before the horse. Instead of focusing solely on the subject of making money, you need to focus on your talents, passions, and plain ol' good ideas so the money will come. You want to get good at this to create the freedom you believe more money will bring to your life.

When contemplating or working on your passions outside of work, what does your product or service do to make lives better? Don't forget that the people who have managed to do this successfully are just like you. The only difference is that they took continuous action. Give yourself the opportunity to be a doer and see how far you go. Sometimes you have to go out on a limb to get the fruit.

Libby's Experience: Your side hustle is usually something you're passionate about. My first side hustle is teaching yoga on Sundays. It is actually one of the best times of my week, because I love sharing my favorite quotes and spending time with my students.

Try to see what you can do to make your life easier, what brings you true happiness. Don't quit your day job . . . yet. This is your primary income. Here is how you can start planning for your side hustle: think about five things you really love doing. When you find those five things, see how you can actually make them into something that generates money. If you like public speaking, maybe you can be a motivational speaker or public-speaking coach. If you want to help someone, maybe life coaching is your deal. *This is your side hustle*. Whatever you do, my word of advice is to certify yourself. This can help you in case of any legal issues. After all, you are trying to make extra money, not lose money. See what resources are out there for you to start the side hustle.

Money Magic: How Much Do You Owe The Man?

Are you in debt? Well, are you? Payback is a you-know-what, but it has to happen. Forget all that extra saving and calculated spending if you still have debt. The interest rate is likely larger than what you'll earn in the stock market and definitely more than your savings account. This means you're bleeding money. You have to stop the leak first, so take most of your savings and future earnings and come up with a plan for paying off debt. Student loans are included here too. Since it seems like it will take forever to pay down debt. It becomes an annoying roommate that you can't shake. Imagine how far along you could be if you ate out less and moved to a cheaper place. Every dollar counts when your life is on fire. Yes, fire! Act like this is an emergency to give it top priority in your financial life.

Plastic Is No Good For You

Pay off your debt. We don't understand why it's so easy for us to get credit cards in college. Then it gets even easier when you get a job. Credit card companies are our worst enemies, except when they give you good things. Some credit cards have rewards, like cash back or airline miles. Others have nothing. If you have a nothing credit card, pay that one off the fastest.

Credit Card Friends And Enemies

Libby's Experience: There are several credit cards that tempt me: the Southwest card, the Chase Sapphire card, and the American Express Hilton card. Those guys are all my best friends and also my worst enemies. My plan of action is to only use one credit card for gas. That's your gas budget, so you can clearly see what amount you're spending. The same card can also be used for all your bills. Do not use this credit card for anything other than your necessary expenses. Credit card number two is used only for your fun expenses. Oh boy, have we opened up a can of worms here. This credit card is only used for your dinners, your movie tickets, and anything and everything that's not a dire need. This will help you see what you are spending on all things.

All right, I'm gonna level with you here. You can have one more like the Southwest and/or American Express Hilton—that way you're getting a two-in-one deal. Only use those when you are booking a flight through Southwest or a Hilton hotel room. Try use these cards only for that specific purpose. Ideally, if you don't use it in a year, I would just close the account so you're not paying the annual fees.

Question: What Would You Do With An Extra 25,000?

Answer: Pay Off Students Loans And Use The Remaining $12 At Brunch

Whether you're a recent grad or have been out of school for ten years, student loans can give you that "'til death do us part" feeling—and not in a good way. They take over a decent amount of your budget and can cause anxiety. It's hard to be thankful for the opportunity to pay for an education when you feel bogged down once you graduate. Plus, we started our careers during a recession! Don't fear: paying down student loans can be daunting, but it's a systematic process that has to be done. By now this debt feels comfortable, and you're ready to settle in and make it a part of your regular life, but stop! Have you looked at refinancing? Try to get a better interest rate and consolidate. Come up with a plan that allows you to successfully pay off the loan with a little more personal sacrifice. If you feel that you would rather put your money towards growing your investments and pay minimums on the loans for now, make sure you are actually investing those funds. But always have a plan. You purchased your education and promised to pay it back, so continue to take responsibility for those actions and feel great about the education you were able to receive.

Sign up for an app that tracks your money and investments. The good and the bad will show up and let you know how well you've done every time you log in. Some will even let you know if your investment allocation could use some adjusting or if you're paying too much in fees. We use both Personal Capital and Mint.com. Setup is easy and free. Tracking your financial future is priceless.

The Basic Of Managing Money Well

Make sure that you're not spending more than you're saving. You need that rainy-day fund. You never know what will happen in this day and age. There are layoffs. We have risks we want to take and entrepreneurial aspirations. All of this takes time, effort, and most importantly, money. You just can't do it without money.

Libby's Experience: Take a good look at your spending. Is it really necessary, or is it something that just makes you happy for a second? I am the worst at buying things when someone pisses me off. That's it, guys—it's the truth. If you make me mad, I will probably buy a watch or purse or even a piece of furniture. I'm sure half of my spending is part of my anger management. Don't fall into that category. That purse will only make you happy for a short time, and then after that, it's associated with the reason you bought it. When you are upset, do me a favor: just put some money in your savings account. A month later, you'll look at how many times you were upset, and then you'll see how much you saved. Get it? Got it? Good! Trust me.

LESSONS LEARNED IN OUR 30S:

1. Everything you read above and more.

#BossWoman

Do I Have To Go To Work?

*L*ibby's Experience: It's 6:00 a.m., and the snoozing dance with the alarm clock has started. Just five more minutes, then four more minutes, and I finally panic and run to the bathroom. I have to get to work by 8:00 a.m. and it's 7:15! I need an extra ten minutes to catch up on Snapchat, Facebook, Twitter, and Instagram. Finally, I have to read the Skimm before the internet security gods take over my phone's freedom at work. Do I really have to go to work today?

If this sounds like your morning dialogue, it might be time to shake things up a little. How many hours does it really take to get ready for work? Try this out: List all the activities you have to do that are work related

Sample Tasks and Hours:

Tasks	Hours Spent	# of Days	Total Hours	
Work	10	5	50	
Morning Prep	1.5	5	7.50	
Commute	2	5	10	
Food Prep and Eating	1.5	5	7.50	
			Total Time:	75 hours

You might say, "I spend seventy-five hours each week just for work, including prep time and transportation. That's a lot of hours!" Make those hours count and meaningful for you. Most people work forty hours a week; truthfully, that's just the minimum. We spend around 30 percent of our lives at work. That means 30 percent of our emotional well-being depends on the career choices we make. But when you consider that the other 70 percent of our lives (30 percent spent sleeping and 40 percent awake and not at work) is conducted outside of work, surely this plays a larger, more important role in our overall happiness. The key is work/life balance. Working too many hours or being under too much stress can impact your personal life and make you unhappy.

Many of us are unhappy with our nine-to-five jobs, and the top five reasons for dissatisfaction are the following:

- Money
- Work stress
- Unfulfilling work
- Not being committed to the job
- Working too much

It's important to address what is making you unhappy and to fix it immediately.

I'm The Boss Of Me

Being your own boss is not related to how the pay system works but to how your thought system works. At the end of the day, your true goal is to be your company's MVP (Most Valuable Player). This is what will help establish whether you are just performing tasks at a job or building the foundation for a career path.

There was a television show years ago called *Who's the Boss?* It was more focused on Tony, the housekeeper (employee), as the main character than the boss (employer). That's exactly the perspective you should have when at your job. You are the main character regardless of your position or title at work. How you look at what you do for a living determines your mind-set on whether it's a just job or a career.

According to Webster's dictionary, a job is "a paid position of regular employment" while a career is "an occupation undertaken for a significant period of a person's life and with opportunities for progress." See the difference?

This mentality is what drives the person's attitude and performance at his or her workplace. Every position is a job; however, the thought process that tends to run through our minds is that I need enough money to eat, pay bills, and other critical aspects in life. So I will have to do what it takes to make a living. This doesn't have to be so black and white; especially nowadays, everyone likes a little bit grey. Sometimes even Fifty Shades of Grey. I (Libby) had to put in a reference of my favorite book series!!

The way you look at your job in your thirties is different from your twenties. A job, on the surface level, often fills a gap for a particular period. A career is something a person specifically trains for and hopes to grow and remain in for his or her working life. However, no matter the job, it should never be taken for granted. If you are feeling that it's a struggle to go to work, it just might be time to reevaluate if this is your career or just a job for now. There is nothing wrong with this struggle. It happens all the time. It's not just you! It's us, too. This is because you probably have been at your job for about three years, and now you are feeling pretty comfortable. No challenges. You have mastered all the skills for this position, and you are ready for the next step. This is when the job itch occurs.

The number one reason people stay at a job is for the MONEY! We love money! The more money the better.

But one day, when you feel content and the need for more money goes away, there will be no searching for the next position. You will seem relaxed with less worries and stress. That's when you know you have found your true calling, also known as your career. You will be happy at what you do for a living and always willing to go the extra mile. Late nights, weekend work, any outside-of-normal work hours will not bother or matter to you. As mentioned before, if you are getting a job itch, change is just around the corner.

House Of Cards

This is the easier path: looking for a job within the same company. Chat openly with your boss about your career development plan; tell her or him your aspirations. If you see a position within the organization, talk to the hiring manager of the job to first express your interest and see if your current skill set will be a match for the position. Then talk to your boss about the opportunity as soon as possible and be honest about why you are interested in this new position.

Your current manager will support your next steps in your career. A good boss understands that you will eventually move on to another position. Meet with the Human Resources (HR) representative to discuss your interest in the position. They will also help with the salary discussions and starting dates. That's always the tricky, sticky part. It's nice to have a coach on your side. Open communication is the best tactic to use when applying for an internal position. It is respectful for everyone involved. Discuss a fair transitional period where you are willing to do the two roles at the same time for a short duration. This helps with the gap in your old position. Finally, make sure that your performance and attitude continue to be excellent throughout the process. Maintain a good relationship with your previous boss and coworkers, even after accepting the new position.

Burning Bridges

So you don't mind burning bridges because you know how to swim. Keep in mind that you never know whom you'll have to manage or who will manage you down the road. The coworker you cursed out several years ago when you were twenty-seven has come back around like a boomerang. And she's sitting in her new office next to your cube, ready to give you hell. She will not have read this book, so she's going to continue to act up, and it'll be your job to make awkward peace with her. This is a situation that you can see and experience. But what about the ones you cannot?

Jillian's Experience: I had a cocky, brash boss when I first started working as a professional. She would speak to me only if I looked nice that day (in my opinion) or if she needed something from me. While she wasn't terrible, she definitely wasn't the ideal leader of the troops. Well, about four years later when she applied to be a manager at a different company where I now worked, I was asked to summarize my experience with her. So what do you think

I said? In our thirties we are more aware of the power of relationships. We're also in better positions to do professional favors for those we like.

Adios!

This is the second path and the harder one, both mentally and physically, because you have decided to leave the company for another job. This is very common nowadays. It's rare for an employee to stay in a job for more than five to ten years. There seems to be a limit, and you definitely know when it is reached. However, it takes time and dedication outside of your normal work hours. That's right: OUTSIDE OF NORMAL WORKING HOURS! Most people need the biweekly paychecks. This is why they keep working until accepting the next job offer.

Also, companies are looking for people who are currently working; they want to interview and hire only the best employees. When you have a job, the potential company is pursuing after you. This is to your advantage. It's not all chocolate-covered strawberries, though. You have to use discretion. The rumors can start by just hearing you express the job itch, and you never know if your current company may start making plans for your departure without letting you know. Rule of thumb: people notice more than you think.

Direct your search for growth in your career and not just a title or position. How will this new job benefit you in the next five years? Keep your job search to yourself. Sometimes it's best to keep our own secrets. That being said, we do have a caveat: start building career-related mentor relationships outside your company. This will give you an excellent sounding board and adviser during these times. Also be open and honest with the future employer on your desire to keep the job search confidential. If references are required, do not list your current boss or coworkers.

Libby's Experience: I was approached recently for a new position, and it was definitely the next step for my career path. I was interested in learning more about the opportunity and interviewing for the position. The hardest part of this process was scheduling the phone conversations and interviews.

Since I worked nine to ten hours a day, I scheduled my conversations with the potential employer during my lunch hours, after work, and even on vacation time. I once had an interview in an airport baggage claim with a drug dog walking around. It was memorable. This was only allowed and understood because of the upfront conversations I had with the potential employer on having interviews before or after regular business hours. They appreciated the integrity that I displayed for my current employer.

Go to a coffee shop or Barnes and Noble, and then dedicate an hour for the job search and application. Leave after the hour; you don't want to get overwhelmed or burned out on your job search.

Recognize when it's time to make a move BEFORE you get disgruntled. That attitude will slow you down and make it harder to move within your company (reputation) or outside of the company (reputation and mental road blocks). Get back on LinkedIn and start making connections like crazy. Start attending those networking mixers that you've been too tired to check out.

78% On The Dollar

If the only thing keeping you from enjoying your current job is the pay, there's a solution for that ... and probably an app. In your twenties you accepted those entry-level jobs that did not allow you to negotiate. Or maybe you were so excited about getting that new job that you didn't want to ruin the moment with the stress of asking for more. Income inequality has been a hot topic for several years, and stats are showing that it may not only be a product of discrimination. We ladies are choosing not to negotiate or just aren't asking for enough. If a job is offered to both you and an equally qualified man at $90K, the salary probably has a range of negotiation between $90K-$105K. Trust me, the HR rep expects you to negotiate; it's already built into the numbers. If you feel that you can ask what the acceptable range entails, and find a fair price in an open conversation, then try to do so. Why does it have to feel like it's you against the company when it comes to your salary? Studies show that men feel more confident and expectant when requesting more money. We are powerful, capable women who should know our worth and the value we bring to the company's table. We are responsible for ourselves and once our salary is set, it is what all raises and bonuses will be based upon. More often than not, an extra several thousand dollars in your pocket will not make or break the company, and it's usually not until you're settled in that you realize it. And don't forget to ask for more vacation, equity, and relocation funds. Sometimes this is overlooked, and that's definitely not good.

Jillian's Experience: I didn't begin to add an extra week into my job negotiations until I was thirty-one. At my previous jobs, I accepted the two weeks offered because it wasn't something I thought of as part of the discussions. I was all about the dollars until I spoke with a colleague about his frequent vacations and realized the truth. He was surprised when I told him I only had two weeks of vacation compared to his three weeks. I had missed a great opportunity to have more time for myself.

Something else I've learned in recent years is that people aren't as bothered by your requests as you think they are. When I changed positions at my job, I received a five percent raise. I accepted it without any negotiations because I knew I was in the middle of the salary range for the position. I worried about what my new boss would think if I asked for more and if I would "price myself out" in coming years by being on the high side of the range. I thought about how I wasn't experienced at this position and would have to start from scratch. A month into my job, he moved to a different department, and I later realized that he did not call the salary shots anyway. In hindsight, he was more concerned with getting his new position and was not concerned about what I asked for. I created an entire story of struggle and strife that did not apply! Undoubtedly, that assumption was from my experiences in my twenties that I hadn't shaken off.

Always A Student

Continue to develop your skills as if you're competing against a twenty-two-year-old. We've seen four-year-olds master the iPad in less than an hour, so watch out for them, too. This is especially important if you've sworn off any additional formal education. Try learning something every six months. While your new talent doesn't have to be work related, this is the Career section, so that's where we will focus. Some relevant classes are Technical Writing, Personal Finance (for those paychecks), Leadership, and anything from the Dale Carnegie Institute. Also, check out online sites like Lynda, Udemy, and Codecademy.

Don't forget your local college has individual continuing education courses you can attend. We are not usually enthusiastic about extra work for ourselves. But it is solely to benefit you and your place in life. If you're not, you are automatically falling behind. You may not see it now, but it's happening. It's the job you wanted but never applied for. We can't coast in our thirties.

Working The Room

By now you have realized that the corporate world is a game, so let's make sure we're on the winning side. Those skills you just acquired from the paragraph above will only get you so far. Being sociable and having a dash of charisma is the magic that seals the deal. If you have been at your company for a few years, you've likely moved up in rank or have big plans to start. Some of your co-workers have already started their upward climb. Even the resident slacker Steve is aiming for higher places. And you're not sure why you and everyone else likes slacker Steve or how he still has a job here. Steve has charisma. He always appears to be socializing instead of doing actual work.

Charisma is learned, so don't worry, you got this. First, listen closely to others. It's about making them feel special, not you. And by listen, we mean actively. So no interrupting to tell your similar story and no thinking about what you want to say while they're speaking. It is engaging in conversation and learning about the other person in a way that makes them feel open and free. Make sure you do it with confidence. This means no beating yourself up, responding negatively, or showing evidence of shyness in your posture and facial expressions. Confidence is being unapologetically okay with whatever you say and do.

Next, you need to be able to generate a quick response according to Dr. Bill von Hippel, the lead researcher and a professor of psychology at the University of Queensland in Australia. Your mental speed might be a little tougher to come by if you don't have it already, but you can make up for that with a bit of attitude. Lastly, get out there and mix it up! We have found that there is comfort in knowing someone as your equal before they become your boss or get a bit of status. You don't have to be as close as cousins, but getting to the level of acquaintance places them in your circle. It's also inspiring to witness their upward movement, which pushes you to do more for your own career. As mentioned earlier, you never know whom you'll have to manage or who will manage you.

Being liked and spreading your social butterfly wings will give you more connections and therefore more options. In our twenties we know how to kiss up and show our eagerness and how to keep our head down and grind. But what we didn't realize is that we are expanding our networks. How far we go in one direction can be based on a handshake from a year ago. For example, your old coworker just moved to the company across the street to manage another department. She can now take you with her! Maybe you don't want to leave now, but next year you could get the itch. This takes a few years to realize because we are all still getting situated in our twenties and making friends with reckless abandon. It may not occur to you that these are the building blocks that help you make your next move.

Will You Be My Mentor?

Mentors are experienced advisors that help make positive changes in another person's life. The key to a mentorship relationship is clear and continuous communication. This will be the only way that mentors can know if there is progress for the mentee.

Forbes has great advice on creating a successful mentorship:

6 Tips to a Successful Mentorship

1. Know What You're Looking for in a Mentor. The first step in finding a mentor is knowing what you want in a mentor.

2. Find a Mentor Who Is Active in the Industry. Look for a business mentor/coach from within the industry you're operating in or aspiring to join—and particularly within organizations/companies you already work with or would like to work with in the future.

3. Make Your Smartest Friend Your Mentor. Schedule a weekly call, and keep each other on track. Make this a priority, and make sure you have an agenda for this call.

4. Make Your Travel Buddies Your Mentors. The friends you travel with can be the most valuable mentors: Finding retreats that allows you to form real bonds with like-minded people and start building the co-mentor relationship.

5. Understand the Mentor's Style. How open-minded are they? How worldly? How do they speak, write, and present themselves as professionals? But really the most important things to assess are fit and trust. Does it feel good to interact with the mentor? Have they achieved things that can

accelerate the entrepreneur's path? Can they impart wisdom that will make a lasting difference to the person being mentored?

6. Know the Difference Between a Mentor and a Coach. Mentoring is largely reactive, whereas coaching can be proactive as often as reactive.

The Challenge: Use your experiences being mentored to become a mentor!

Libby's Experience: Being a female engineer was, and still is, a rare commodity. You need your sisterhood of traveling engineers or traveling mentors. It's comforting to have someone guiding and advising me on my next steps. Now, after spending a decade in my field, it's time to be a mentor. Pay it forward! This is one of my favorite aspects of working with colleges and high schools. Being a mentor is my gift to the mentees. It's an opportunity to share my experiences and answer any questions they may have. I recently joined a mentorship program called Glassbreakers. Their algorithm uses professional and personal details to introduce you to peers with similar career goals.

#Vacay

Along with being a hard worker and sometimes even a workaholic, you need to take vacations. Take as many lengthy or mini-vacations as you can throughout the year. You deserve to see the world, or in Libby's case, make four trips to New York. It's no joke to say that we are overworked and sometimes even burned out. Vacations are the break you are craving.

The benefits of taking some time off are numerous:

- A mental break from your daily routine
- A different perspective when you take a step away.
- You are taking care of yourself.

Space out your vacation days. You have to make them last for the WHOLE YEAR. Below are some suggestions for people like Libby who only have two weeks. (P.S. I forgot to negotiate for an extra week during my job interview as well!)

- Three-day weekend vacations (either taking off Friday or Monday).
- Four-day weekend vacation (take off Friday and Monday).
- Seven-day extended week (leave Friday night, take the entire week off, return the following Sunday). This is a total of five days of vacation used.

My personal favorite: the random one-day vacation during the week.

My Company

Why haven't you started your own business? Are you looking for the perfect idea, or do you have one already? Working as an employee is a common path but it does not have to be yours. Every day that we go to work as employees, we are helping someone else realize their dream and taking life away from our own. What are the things keeping you from getting started on your goal of being your own boss? Write it down so you can see these reasons unfold and easily pick them apart. Next, stop being afraid to fail. It gives you a chance to relieve yourself of undue pressure and helps you get started. The key here is to start. You don't need to wait until you lose five pounds, learn Spanish or ask fourteen people. You can literally just start. Remember, failure is learning. and often a stepping stone to success.

LESSONS LEARNED IN OUR 30S:

1. Be the MVP at work.
2. Be discrete when searching for a new job.
3. Enjoy your job!
4. Take Mini-Vacations.

#Contacts

*You are the average of the five people you spend the
most time with.*

—*Jim Rohn, motivational speaker*

y now we have seen many a friendship flourish, fade, and flourish again. It's part of that natural ebb and flow of people in our lives. We need to evaluate our lineup of current friends and be aware of their influence. In the land of thirty-somethings, let's keep in mind that true friendships are still necessary, and meeting new people is good and healthy.

Jillian's Experience: You may have experienced a life event making you a candidate for finding new friends that share your current situation or location. After relocating for a new job, I had the opportunity to find new like-minded people to call my friends. My go-to tactic was to get on the young professionals circuit and head to their next social event. Just Google "young professionals" to find these groups online. You never know who you'll meet: maybe even your future husband. Libby has seen it happen. Just make sure you commit to attending multiple events.

Mind-Set: For New Friendships

Don't assume everyone has their social circle figured out. It's an excuse to be timid or indolent. With that said, there are people singing Drake's "No New Friends" who will not embrace you the way you envisioned.

Jillian's Experience: There was a point in my life where I was only interested in hanging with my select group of friends and didn't have even the slightest urge to branch out. It was a fun and comfortable feeling to know there was one less mission in life to work on. And once I sank deep into my cushion of friendship, one of the seams began to rip as two of my closest buddies moved away for grad school and a better job, respectively. Another friend mastered online dating and now has a steady boyfriend. You see where this is going? I probably met several people who were great potential friends but never dug deeper because I was set, albeit temporarily. I now welcome new friends in my life regardless of how comfortable my friendship cushion may be. Yes, I talk to strangers! Studies show that conversations with strangers bump up your level of happiness. These can be bite-sized chats about something funny or long, Starbucks chats that turn into subsequent friendships. We humans have a thing for connecting with others, so don't deny yourself the pleasure.

Every person that you see is not an enemy until proven friendly. Remember the girl across the room that looked like your new imaginary arch nemesis until you spoke to her and realized she's your spirit animal? And didn't you feel a little silly that you branded her as Darth Vader and wasted those moments not having her in your life? If everyone was a potential friend the moment you set your eyes on them, you'd have a much larger network of friends and opportunities right this minute! Make it a practice of believing that everyone you come across loves you and wants to have fun. Not everyone will stop what they're doing at the sight of you and ask you to be in their flash mob dance routine (are people still doing those?). It's not about them being super receptive to you; it's about you relaxing and being open to others. You can't control their actions, but you can prevent yourself from being part of the problem.

How Many Friends Should You Have?

When it comes to your health and happiness, you should first know that Facebook and Twitter friends don't amount to much when compared to friends who are present. Studies show that you should have between three and five close friendships for your wellbeing. It's okay to even have one very close friend with whom you share your ups and downs.

Jillian's Experience: Honestly, it would be difficult to juggle more than five BFFs. I've found that my three closest friends are enough. They have been with me for eight to twenty years, and I am so thankful for attracting such wonderful people into my life. Nowadays, we have our own stuff going on and staying up all night gabbing without a second thought now requires a third thought. We crave those quiet moments that make up alone time because we are working at the office, running errands, and going to bed a lot earlier. We want to get out and be a part of civilization but can't seem to get off the couch. "The best plans are cancelled plans" is one of my favorite sayings.

Do You Have Enough Friends To Invite To Your Party?

Robin Dunbar, an anthropologist and evolutionary psychologist states that you can keep track of 150 friends and acquaintances before your memory gives out. It comes from the ancient days when villages consisted of about 150 people because it gave them a sense of community. I know many of us are saying, "150 people? I can't get to 50!" But let this be part of the jump-start you need to meet more people. But don't hurt yourself trying to get to 150 friends. You'll be fine either way.

Remember the friend who helped you get a job or the one who encouraged you to try pilates? We all need good people in our lives. These are the people that influence and inspire. They open the doors of your mind (and actual doors) and help you lift yourself to a new level. Seek out friendships with people you want to emulate. They should be passionate about life and possess something that you want to improve within yourself. If you aren't very creative but want to be, befriend people who are. If you have your own business, choose people that have one as well, and then choose the successful business owners amongst them. This should not be done with the intention of taking advantage of people for your own personal gain. You should not stalk these people online with the sole purpose of using them to get ahead. In fact, when you are making new friends you should be thinking about actions you can take to improve their lives, not yours..

Make a connection and invite them out for coffee later if they have a good vibe and could be fun to hang out with. If you aren't getting the friendship vibes from them, you can always put them in the acquaintance box. The point here is to connect with people whom you have something in common, so you can better each other and have a few laughs along the way. And what you have in common can include career, money, spiritual, or creative goals, to name a few.

You may ask yourself, "Why is there so much emphasis and pressure put on meeting all of these people? I've gotten this far without a gazillion friends and associates, and I'm content." The reality is that there are experiences you are missing that you never knew you could have. There's an opportunity cost (remember calculating that in college?) associated with choosing to interact with less people.

Keeping Up Friendships

At our age we have had friends relocate, get married, or have babies, and may find ourselves grasping at friend straws. This doesn't mean you have to give up on anyone who is no longer like you. At this time in our lives we are more selective with whom we reveal our secret love for adult coloring books. Staying in touch with confidants keeps those quality friendships going.

We think the hardest part of friendship these days is keeping them. You're working late (again), or you have a free weekend, but you're too exhausted to meet up. Or, you only have fifteen minutes to talk to your friends, but the story you're going to tell them will take a full hour, including analysis and problem solving. So you don't call.

If you take a closer look at your schedule, you'll realize that keeping up friendships is likely near the bottom of your priority list. Invite a friend to go running with you, or work through lunch so you can attend happy hour. Have the girls over for dinner since you planned to eat that night anyway. You will work on the things you value, so instead of sitting around feeling guilty for not keeping in touch, feel the joy of being in the present moment with a loved one. Make time, not excuses.

Our advice is to not worry about who's single, who's married, who's divorced, and who now has kids. What matters is that all these people are your friends. It's natural for your friends that are married and have children to spend more time with people sharing that same lifestyle. Their lives have changed. That's okay. They might not be your everyday friends, but they are still there for you.

Once you have started making more time for your friends, you may find that some are not who you think they are. They might be going through changes that are making them harder to love and aren't interested in making improvements. These friends usually range from haters to beraters and will push you to reevaluate those friendship contracts. Or they might have found someone that relates to them better and have chosen to spend less time with you. Whatever the reason, things are moving in a different direction.

Give it the ol' college try and see if you can get things back on track. Have that discussion or don't. We've experienced this since our days on the playground, but our fourth decade has us equipped with more focus and the confidence we need to be okay with the outcome and move on. Don't try to force anything because effort should be met with effort. They may resurface and rekindle the friendship after taking some time to grow and sort through their own life. Support them from afar, and get back to the friends that are there for you.

Letting Go of Friendships
You are NOT being rude.
You are NOT being mean.
You ARE controlling your own time.

Libby's Experience: I was a huge social butterfly. I wanted all the friends in the world. The more friends on Facebook, the better. I would wake up Saturday morning and call the world, my world. I was the person that you hung out with on Friday night and would be ready on Saturday morning to recap about Friday night (less than four hours ago). I would talk on the phone for hours.

All of that changed in my life, when my dad passed away in 2013. I lost a part of myself and just wanted to be alone. I couldn't be that motivating, Indian Oprah for my friends. I just didn't want to respond to the question, "How are you doing?" I couldn't be the person who calls everyone anymore. My goal was to keep going and to never look back on that day with anyone else. I did lose several friends. It's really hard to help someone when they're going through something so tragic and life changing. It's very natural for somebody to back away and hope that eventually your friendship will be back to normal. Sometimes it will never be back to normal: it's just your new normal.

At the end of the day, everybody in our life makes an impact whether they're friends for life or friends for the day. Embrace life for what it gives you. Always say thank you because you never know why that person came into your life and why they left. That is a question that may never be answered.

Family Ties

As we get older we value our family time and appreciate that we have more in common with them as experienced adults. Our thirties are a great time to start having those conversations that we would not have been comfortable discussing in our twenties. Family stories of love, loss, secrets and dreams unfold more easily and with greater understanding. It's like a graduating from the kids table (again).

Libby's Experience: On my favorite TV shows, *ABC's The Bachelor and The Bachelorette*, the "hometown dates" are usually closer to the end of the show for the contestants. Usually four out of the twenty-five people make it to meet the family. The contestants are scrutinized on whether their personality and character align with the family dynamics before a final decision is made. This is because we represent our family as they represent us. We are known to be so-and-so's daughter before we create our own identity. They are our foundation. They are our people.

The significance of family was a huge part of my upbringing; however, in my younger days, my parents were not so cool. I didn't get them; they didn't get me. It was an utterly frustrating and confusing situation. Now I realize that my parents are my best friends. Especially my dad. My daddy never let me go to sleep without saying, "I love you." He did not like the thought of going to sleep angry; it wasn't worth it to him. He always said, "We are family and we love each other unconditionally, regardless of any situation. I am always going to be on your side."

Mom is now retired after working for what seems to be a gazillion years. She is the firecracker in our family. She is the size of a mouse with the memory of an elephant and plays the devil's advocate in every single situation in my life. At times I wondered why she took this approach, but then I realized that if she didn't, I may have never seen a situation clearly. While she can be my biggest judge and critic, she is my support system as well. Spending time with your parents now is a gift you may not have later. Mom and I create experiences by going to 3D movies and designing plates at Mad Potter. In my thirties, I realized that it's quality time that matters to the both of us, not the quantity. It is with our family that we ride the roll-ercoaster of life. Family is a gift from God. They're the ones we call when someone takes their first breath, and also the ones we call when someone takes their last. They make life better.

Jillian's Experience: My mom and dad have always been there for me. Growing up it was easier to connect with them in the early stages of my youth. Like most teenagers, I separated from my "lame" parents and start-ed to forge my own identity until I entered adulthood. It was then that I began to fully appreciate them as people, not just parents. It's funny to think back to when I was a child, watching my parent's friends come by for a game of Trivial Pursuit. They were about the same age as I am now, only with children. It made me recognize that they had their own path, friends, fun and first names. Not to mention boring games.

All my life I have had my older sister, Candice, by my side. We're less than two years apart and share the same mindset on most topics. We both have the same quiet disposition but can talk all day about nothing and everything. I value our relationship and love having someone who lived through the same experiences. Sometimes she is the only one that understands me. I mean that literally, since we have our own mumble-y language that no one can decode. She and the rest of my family have been a blessing and our relationships get even better as we age.

LESSONS LEARNED IN OUR 30S:

1. Join a young professional group to meet like-minded people.
2. It's okay with letting go okay with letting go of your friends. Life happens.
3. Be ready to be a friend.
4. Cherish the time with your family.

#LoveStory

On a scale of 1 to 5 (1 being I'm a Pro-dater to 5 being Hold my hand and secretly watch my date from binoculars), What would be your ranking? Would you date yourself? Every love story first begins with you!

Romance Me

Whether on purpose or by accident, you are a party of one. For many of us, this begins to wear thin on our patience, faith, and mood. Every Facebook post you read is about someone getting engaged or married, or it's the sonogram of the child. They are no longer like you. They have different priorities. Feeling left behind much?

On the Sex and the City episode "Bay of Married Pigs," Charlotte knew how we are feeling when she said, "I hate it when you're the only single person at a dinner party, and they all look at you like you're an alien . . .

Around this time, we thirty-somethings dive deep into investigating how smart, attractive, normal people like ourselves have slipped through the marriage cracks. In our twenties, we relied on time to make us feel better. There's less of that now. The old "I want to be ____ before I'm thirty" statement no longer applies. Don't sweat! We have a plan! First start with dating yourself. Ask yourself out on a date.

I've been single for a while and I have to say; it's going very well. Like . . . It's working out. I think I'm the one.

—Emily Heller, standup comedian.

This is the perfect time to find hobbies and new activities on your bucket list. This is a way to prepare yourself for being happy, interesting, and alone or being a happy, interesting person with your future mate. Either way, the end result will equal fun and/or the realization that you can get out there and try new things.

Here are some suggestions for activities you can do:

- Work out.
- Read our book! Wait, you are doing it!
- Sign up for an art, writing, or yoga class.
- Volunteer.
- Travel.
- Visit a museum.
- Watch a play.

We admit, some of these activities will be better suited for introverts and some better for extroverts. You can start by simply going to a movie; a matinee works best and it's cost effective. When feeling self-conscious, pretend you're on a mission or conducting some experiment to make the world a better place. Report back to your friends to make it feel official.

Speaking of making the world a better place, volunteering is a superb way to connect with your community. Serving others makes you forget about serving yourself. It's a great distraction from any drama (or lack thereof) that eats away at your time. You come away from the experience feeling as if you've made a difference, and you probably have. It's also a shortcut to happiness and even meeting new people. Volunteering gives you the opportunity to practice and develop your social skills by meeting regularly with people that have common interests. Once you have momentum, it's easier to branch out and make more friends and contacts.

Currently, we are both part of Junior League in our respective cities. Through this non-profit organization, we have made friends, experienced networking opportunities, and socialized with like-minded people. It gives us a chance to belong to something bigger.

At our former company we were involved in a volunteering program that allowed us to pick and choose different activities such as game night with the senior citizens, patient visits at the hospital during lunch, and festival booth volunteers with the city of Houston. It's a great experience to share with others, and even encourages them to join you. Other places to begin your new life of volunteering are food banks, museums, and places of worship.

After you have been out and about creating meaningful work, it's time to go home and enjoy doing absolutely nothing. We all know that wrapped-up-in-your-blanket-eating-pizza-on-a-rainy-day feeling. You hope the phone stays silent, your laundry isn't spilling over the hamper, and there is nothing that you need to focus on right this minute. So before you start a Netflix binge or go down the internet rabbit hole, just stop and enjoy the quiet. You've had a busy day, and you should cherish this time. Think about the best thing that happened today or something you wish would happen tomorrow. Reflect on how you don't need someone else to be your everything because you are perfectly happy being that person for yourself. No lousy, negative thoughts allowed here. You can only anticipate things that make you smile.

Libby's Experience: You can't truly know what you are looking for until you know yourself. I was at a yoga workshop this past year working on a teaching exercise. One of the girls needed a filler phrase before she moved the class to the next a pose. She stumbled with her thoughts said, "You do you." We all loved it!

So first and foremost, do you find yourself interesting? Would you date yourself? Let's say BJ Novak asked me out on a date; he is the man of my dreams with his witty charm! Would we have an amazing dinner or just an ordinary one? After all, he has also dated the wonderful and talented Mindy Kaling (sister from another mother). My obvious answer is BJ will fall in love with me at first sight and then rush me to De Beers where he proceeds to pick out the best ring for me. All this, after seeing me for three seconds max. Hey, a girl can dream. At the end of the day, even if BJ dated Mindy the obvious fact is that you are you, and that's why people are attracted to you: because you do you.

Now For The Dating Lessons You Expected During This Chapter.

Take Action

When you're out there making these actions your reality, just know that it is easier to date in your thirties than in your twenties. Remember all of the guys you gave chances to-- that should never have been on your radar in the first place? This doesn't happen so easily once you're a thirty-something. Your more focused on finding that person who fits well with you. You know what you want and aren't afraid to quickly move on from what isn't meant to be. It's not just because you are trying to scurry toward the person of your dreams. It's because you've crossed a new threshold of maturity where you become your number one priority (or at least in the top three). You are more self-assured, less self-conscious and the result is a better you.

Do your friends and coworkers know you're single and looking? You never know who they know and how it can help you. Being vocal about your intentions puts it out there in the universe, so things begin to happen. The entire office does not need to know. But how many times have you casually mentioned something and found out that the person you're speaking to can actually help? So don't be afraid to speak up.

You know the saying about how the only person you'll meet at home is the pizza delivery guy? HOME a four-letter word. Make yourself available! You have to get out there so people can see you. How else will they know you exist? In our thirties we tend to slow things down a bit, even when the goals in our lives dictate that we continue to make an effort. We get excited about Friday nights because we get to snuggle up with Hulu. We love Saturday mornings because it's an excuse to stay in bed with the covers over our heads. Saturday nights we have our friends over for games and gossip. On Sunday we only leave the house to run boring errands. What do we do during the week? Go straight home and count down the days until the weekend. Yes, the early thirties see the beginnings of Homebody Syndrome. And it's contagious. All it takes is one friend developing it to spread to the rest of the crew.

So here's what you do. Don't go home! Remember the hobbies you started while dating yourself? Keep them up and add happy hour. Head over to that place that's popular with young professionals. People are more inclined to start a conversation with you when you are alone. If you do choose to bring a group, be sure to separate yourself from them at times and hang out at the bar. Steak houses, restaurants with breweries, and sports bars are great places to find guys. Try farmers' markets, car washes, and popular neighborhood parks, too. And remember that going alone will still yield the best results.

It's not enough to just go to these places. Trust me; you have to be in it to win it. You also need to keep nonverbal communication in mind. Dress for the occasion and make eye contact. If you suffer from RBF (look it up) be aware of this and put a smile on it.

For those rainy days when you're not out and about or just need a break from the outside world, get your profile together for online dating. When making yourself available, you have to think of all the places you can to meet your potential mate. If you think online dating is for geeks and dweebs, then you need to make current events one of your hobbies. It's for everyone now, and the amount of shame and embarrassment felt are way closer to nil these days. Plus, your focus is to meet someone, and that trumps how you think everyone thinks of you anyway. Get to swiping.

Jillian's Experience: I navigated my way through a couple of dating sites in the past. I loved scrolling through all of my dating options from the comfort of my sofa. My best online match was with a smart, funny guy who loved everything that I loved. He was the male version of myself but the timing was not right, as he was moving overseas later that season. My worst online date was with a guy that held me captive for two hours at a popular sandwich shop with boring conversation about his lack of goals. He didn't even offer to get me a cup of water as he sipped his strawberry smoothie. He emailed me later that week asking what he did wrong when I ghosted. I kindly laid it out for him with bullet points and diagrams, you know, as a favor for the next woman that might cross his path.

Libby's Experience: I didn't really date until I was in my twenties. That's right! I didn't date in my teens because I wanted to be the straight-A student and student body president. I wanted to make a change by implementing more rules for everyone. It was the best time of my life. Then I went off to Aggieland to become an engineer. Here is where my dating life really started. I had freedom! I will be first to tell you that I'm not good at dating. It actually scares me to pieces. Sometimes I literally throw up before the date or during the date. Sorry for the gross details, but it's the truth. That's how scared I am of dating: genuinely and utterly petrified. And if I like a guy, to him it probably looks like I hate his guts. However, I try to keep in mind the old adage stating that in order to get rid of your fear, you have to face it.

By my mid-twenties, I was finished with all my education, had an awesome job, and was sure the hubby was just around the corner, along with a puppy. It was like I had all the pieces for my side of the chessboard except for my King piece. If only finding him was like Amazon Prime shipping! I'm kidding, but seriously, how great would that be? My momentum of dating picked up after college. I did some online dating and singles events, but there was always the fear of rejection.

Date 2 Date

Practice dating. Like any pro athlete, one does not become an overnight success story. There is always something else that happens before, and it's always their perseverance and determination that gets them the win! The first step is to say yes to every date that was introduced by a friend. The second step is to say yes to everyone with whom we have common interests. Let's be real: the last step is to say yes to all cute guys! We all love our eye candy. Isn't that why we watched Magic Mike? It's a never-fail algorithm.(winky face)

As we write this charming, mind-blowing section on dating, we are still single! In our twenties, we just wanted to have fun and learn how to date. We have met some really awesome people who have taught us a lot about life, as well as dating. (If you, dear reader, happen to be one of these guy friends, you should skip to the next section)! LOL, we are joking! Please keep reading.) As we were saying, now we are dating with the intention of finding our future husbands. So we don't drag out dates anymore. We want to meet multiple people and use the process of elimination. It worked on standardized test; it's a methodical approach.

It is possible that guys we have dated in the past may take offense, but now we are looking for our life partners (that's what Libby's daddy used to call it). It's not the same as swiping left and right. You can start that way, but don't waste your time on the people who don't value yours. Think of doctors' offices and salons, if you don't show up for your appointment, you can still be charged. They might let you reschedule, but it probably won't be free. In other words, you should put a value on your time. How much is a minute or two, or an hour, of your time worth? The rule of thumb still applies to regular dating and online dating. Be safe. Make sure you meet in a public place. Don't do anything that you wouldn't normally do; go with your gut reaction. Your gut reaction is accurate most of the time!

Libby's Experience: As I mentioned before, dating is not my forte, and I'm such a scaredy-cat that I even valet park my car so there is no murder scene when the guy tries to walk me to my car after the date. I think your intuition tells you a lot, and you just have to take a deep breath and figure out whether it feels right. It's okay if it does cause a little heartbreak; this, too, will pass.

When you date multiple people at a time, you wind up creating a lot of friendships. Naturally, the ghosting phenomenon takes place for the rest of guys. But it all depends on your relationship with the person. It seems that modern dating appreciates ghosting more than the "it's not you, it's me" talk.

Goodbye And Good Luck

First, let's remember you always have options. We all know these signs and red flags; however, it's always nice to have reminders.

1. He never calls, only texts.
2. He doesn't plan anything ahead of time. It's always a last-minute thing.
3. He is not romantic.
4. He does not try to impress you.
5. He does not introduce you to his friends after five dates or a month of dating.
6. He doesn't ask about your family or friends.
7. He does not return you calls or text within twenty-four hours.
8. This list can just keep going and going. We already know these things and more.

Just say, BYE 4EVER!

BAE –Got The Guy?

Being with that special guy in your life makes everything better, doesn't it? Having someone to love is wonderful, fun, and freeing. Not to mention, you get to check off one of those Life Goals boxes. So what's next? Since we are more stable and focused outside of our twenties, we have a shorter dating period, and marriage talk comes up more often. We are dating for marriage, after all! In general, it takes longer for us ladies to fall in love, and there are qualities in a man that we have found to carry more weight compared to our twenty-something self:

- respectful
- established
- generous
- low-key
- planner
- family-minded
- romantic

Are these qualities important in our twenties? Yes! But back then we also spent more time falling for men with the potential-to-be-potential, bad boys, and men we liked only because they showed us some attention. It didn't matter so much that they were still learning to be gentlemen, couldn't pay rent, and were sloppy kissers. Now that you found BAE you have to do your part to make sure the sun is always shining.

I, Jillian, am a certified homebody who loves to date homebodies. It's awesome! We love binge-watching television shows and ordering takeout. How many days can we do this in a row? We don't know because one of us will suggest going for a walk, dancing, or a festival after a day or two keep things fresh. I can recognize a rut a mile away and will try not to get stuck in it whenever possible. The added benefit of finding different types of activities is having even more stuff to talk about and the great memories you get to post on Instagram! Here are some tips for maintaining a great relationship:

A great rule of thumb when you are in a committed relationship is to pretend that you are both still dating so that you'll continue to do your hair and make-up and not gain the "Relationship 15." Still flirt and find ways to touch and be intimate. Listen to him. Remember when you used to just listen? Put on your "get him" dress instead of your "got him" dress. Only wear your fancy sweats when hanging out on the couch. You get what we're saying here? Make him feel special, loved, and wanted by you.

Jillian's Experience: I have found that my conflict resolution skills have gotten better as I've aged. When I was involved in heated discussions with someone I was dating, the goal was always to win. This meant he had to lose. Plus, I am a very logical person and never wrong. But somewhere down the line, I realized that if this is the person I have chosen to love and support, I shouldn't want him to be a loser at anything. This changed the way

I conducted myself in arguments and opened my ears to understanding his perspective.

Resurrect those friends you had before you fell off the map. Give some attention to those hobbies you took on earlier in this chapter. Couples that stay together don't always have to play together. In fact, it's healthy to have your own life outside of the relationship. Missing your man creates excitement when you finally see each other again. And, of course, that feeling is reciprocated. Plus, we all appreciate a person who has passion(s) and activities in their life. Your partner is not exempt.

Make time for each other. If you're DINK (Dual Income No Kids) or DINKY (Dual Income No Kids Yet), you should be traveling or finding other new ways to create memories and joyful experiences. A road trip down the Cali coast, a winery tour, or a lunch date on a Tuesday will do you some good. Trust us.

Keep it spicy like a habanero. If you can't get there, aim for jalapeño. Buy that lingerie and light those candles! This is more important than you may know, and keeping it up will make you both happier.

Air your grievances as they come. You are going to have those moments when you don't even want to be in the same room, but make sure you let your guy know what he did that has you glum. Start the sentence with "I feel" instead of "You" to keep blame and the resulting defensiveness from ruining a good discussion. You are in charge of your own happiness, so ensure that you don't stay glum by ruminating over the negative parts.

Do the work! Make this relationship top priority. Repeat all of the above as necessary, and believe us, they are necessary. The reason relationships grow stale is because we stop creating those wonderful moments. Make sure you're doing your part by staying inspired and action oriented.

Give gifts that are unforgettable and create memories for a lifetime. The associate pastor at Libby's church recently mentioned a story about how his now-wife once gave him twelve special dates for Christmas as a gift. He realized later that this meant that she wanted to spend the entire next year with him. He proposed to her that year!

LESSONS LEARNED IN OUR 30S:

1. Date yourself.
2. Start checking things off on your bucket list. New hobbies! New adventures!
3. Be open to meeting people.
4. Don't stay in a relationship if it's not for LOVE.
5. Let your guy know that he is only for you and you alone.

See You Later

So we have come to the conclusion of our book. You learned so much about us and our opinions, as well as the many resources available to you. There is an endless number of serious and/or fun topics we discuss, and the reference materials are extensive. Our goal was to grab the major subjects (Beauty, Body, Meals, Fashion, Money, Career, Friendships, and Relationships) that are important to women in their thirties and share that information with you all.

We are regular women sharing daily experiences and hope that our book is something you will give to your girlfriends, family members, mentors, and mentees. Maybe even your husbands. Our book will hopefully start many conversations for you guys. After all, that's how our book started. It was a conversation between two best friends about everything! Don't forget to try the challenges in the Appendix, and especially read the bonus chapter. When you do, you will understand why we added the chapter to the end of the book. Feel free to reach us through our social media outlets and emails. It would truly be an honor to hear from you ladies! Check out our website at http://www.lessonsinour30s.com/.

Bonus Chapter:
#AskBelieveReceive

Soul – Searching, Good Juju, And Going Deeper

We wanted to save the best for last. This topic took our friendship from work acquaintances to BFFs! Whether you're religious or not, you've probably had moments where you've pondered your place in this world. You're in your thirties, so you're probably looking for a sense of purpose, inner peace, and more happiness—something to round out your life thus far. Heading to work, going home, and repeating as necessary can leave you asking for that sense of fulfillment and wholeness. In addition, a lot of us have the feeling that we're not living up to society's expectations (you're not married yet?) or missing out on common life events.

We have embarked on this journey over the last several years to make peace with any undesirable situations in which we have been involved. We also try to make peace with the fact we are deserving of what is good and right in our universe. Whether we are praying, meditating, or throwing our hands up, shouting to whoever is listening, we all need to make time for soul searching.

Where Is Oprah When You Need Her?

How do you keep the inner peace in your life? Are you winning and losing or winning and learning? We are firm believers in the law of attraction. This subject has kept us on the phone for hours. The law of attraction states that your thoughts and feelings attract things and situations into your lives. It is a universal law that uses a universal force of energy to which we are all connected.

Many religions, and even physics, reference this law in their own way. Love is the most powerful force of energy and the strongest of our feelings. With this law, like attracts like, and there are no coincidences. You have the power to direct your life, and the law is always working, whether you believe in it or not. Deeeep.

Are You There God? It's Me Libby

Libby's Experience: Has there ever been a time in your life when you are questioning, "When is it my turn? How is this person getting married? Why did this other person get the job I wanted? What is my life supposed to be about?" These are usually my questions to God.

It was not until I read The Secret that I really understood the power of mind over matter. I briefly mentioned it in the body chapter. The mind over matter technique is much bigger than your physical image; it is about shifting your mental image.

If you want to be sad, think of all the depressing events and actions happening in the world, or even in your own life. You might shed a tear or two. If you want to be happy, though, think of the things that put a smile on your face. I love watching Jimmy Fallon's games and interactions with his guests; just watching him makes me LOL. It's like Jimmy and I are best friends that hang out all the time.

The law of attraction references the universe; for me, that's God. I am a very religious person who goes to church every week and says my prayers. I truly believe that God has a plan for everyone. Only recently, I realized that I am co-creating that plan with Him. In the Bible, God clearly states, "Therefore I tell you, whatever you ask in prayer, believe that you have received it, and it will be yours" (Mark 11:24). At first, I wondered if the law of attraction was some kind of hocus pocus. Then, I realized it's how you state your desires. I write letters to

God every day. It is more than a law of attraction method—it's my way of praying.

Try it out. Write a letter of gratitude for what you have in your life. Then, take an additional step. Thank (Him) for your dreams and wishes, as if they came true when you first woke up this morning. Notice the difference in your attitude and your outlook for the rest of the day. This is when you just start seeing changes happen around you.

Sometimes, it's easier to see what your desires are rather than just stating them or thinking about them. Placing pictures that represent your goals on a poster where you can see them may just give you the push to hold yourself accountable to attain them. This is the vision board technique.

#VisionBoardParty

It's time to party with your friends (with a purpose in mind)! Host a vision board party every year in January. Then, throughout the year, you can encourage your friends to achieve their goals.

Here are a couple of helpful hints for your vision boards:

1. Create a focus title.
2. Look in magazines for pictures, take new photos and use ones you already have from your personal photo album.
3. Place the board somewhere you will see it often. Spend time daily looking at the pictures and

> thinking about how you will feel when you have, be, or do what is on the board.

4. Turn visualization into inspired action. Do something related to your desires.

Libby's Experience: I have created several vision boards, and I try to do one at least twice a year. I am always looking for signs. It makes me happy when I see signs, because I feel like they're little miracles from God. I cannot tell you how much reading The Secret has changed my life. I still apply the principals daily by reading the messages from The Secret app on my phone. Many people use the Secret without even knowing it. It's trusting in God, asking for exactly what you want, and believing that you will receive it.

Here's the story about how I became a yoga teacher and how my vision board played a huge part. I did my very first vision board exercise at a business women's conference. I found a picture of lady who was running on hot stones. Fast-forward a couple of months: I signed up to train to be a hot yoga teacher at YogaOne Houston. Note that the specific type of yoga that I teach is HOT Yoga. I truly believe this opportunity had something to do with the intention I set and the picture of the woman running on hot stones.

List It

Another method is to write a list, but write it as if you already have everything you want. Create it in the morning, and then read it before you sleep at night. Writing your wants down and paying attention to the list every day reminds the Universe that you know you will receive these desires soon. The sky is the limit! If you don't write much, try out an activity called zentagle. You can just write words or phrases in between the designs

Clear Visions

Expect all your heart's desires to come true in every area of your life. The power is in our feelings and their strength. When you want something badly, how do you feel about it? Are you excited and expectant of its arrival, or are you anxious and sad that it is not yet here?

Jillian's Experience: Here is a bit of my law of attraction in action. I decided that I was ready for something new position at work. I had launched negative thoughts and feelings about that job into the universe. At the same time, I launched what I did want. Having this negative experience made think about what would bring me satisfaction. I wanted that position across the room that paid more and allowed me flexibility to travel and to work independently. I closed my eyes and visualized sitting next to my new coworkers, and grew more excited with each passing thought. Your mind can't tell what is real versus imagined, so there's power in this process. I also sent positive thoughts to my current position, because being happy where you are shows appreciation and makes you feel even better.

Later, I confided in my coworker about my plans. This is where it got a little discouraging. She said, "It takes forever to get a new position on this floor. Those words inspired me to more love and light into my next move. Don't let people bring you down with stories based on their imagined reality. I started asking those in the position I wanted to explain their jobs in detail and made friendly conversation. Two months later, one of the guys I chatted up sent me a text message that he had just put in his two weeks' notice. Now, here's the part that gets tricky: you have to take action. I told the manager that I wanted the position being vacated by my new friend. Within four months, I was seated next to my new coworker and making jokes with my new boss. I have been to Brazil, Costa Rica, and have road-tripped across the Cali coast without taking a day of vacation time (thanks, flexible schedule!).

Were There Doubts Along The Way?

Yep. We sabotage our own efforts from time to time by giving in to our negative thoughts and not seeing the bigger picture that is our life. We're human and have been taught to expect the worst and hope for the best. Just remember that you have control of your thoughts and, therefore, control of your feelings and experiences, and that's what matters at the end of the day. Share your lists, letters, and visions boards with us using #30sGoals!

Live The Book

The Live the Book section allows us to build a continuous relationship with you, our readers, and further develop the *Lessons In Our 30s* community. The following pages contain one week challenges for all the previous chapters. Our Instagram will have posts related to these challenges so keep a look out! Most importantly enjoy!

Mirror Mirror Challenge
Beauty Prep

Day	Task
1	Clean Your Makeup Brushes
2	Throw Away Expired Makeup and Skincare
3	Visit Dermatologist for Skin Checkup
4	Replace Any Necessary Skincare Items
5	Create Your Own Sugar Scrub
6	Clean Out Makeup Bag
7	Reorganize Beauty Area

Hey Good-Looking
7 Day Morning Workout Challenge
By Clifford Genese

Each Morning Wake Up 20 Minutes Earlier To Perform Exercises Below:

Equipment Needed: yoga mat, interval timer

What to Do: Choose 5 exercises to perform for each morning. Perform each exercise for one minute with no rest in between. If doing multiple rounds, rest 1 minute in between each.

Beginner Level: 1 round
Intermediate Level: 2 rounds
Advanced Level: 3 rounds

Exercises:
Push-ups
Superman
Bridge
Tricep Push-ups
Cross Toe Touch
Alternating Lateral Lunge
Plyometric Squats

Chow Time
No Added Sugar Challenge

Our bodies need natural sugar for fuel but added sugars can lead to health issues.

For 7 days lets kick the added-sugar addiction and get our minds and bodies on the right track.

Rules:	Task
1	Only Natural Sugars from Fruit, Veggies & Dairy
2	No Refined Carbs
3	No Sugary Condiments & Sauces
4	No Sugary Drinks (Including Alcohol)
5	No Artificial Sweeteners

Style Me Challenge
Closet Makeover

Day	Task
1	Pull ALL Items Out of Closet
2	Determine Which Items Will Be Donated or Sold
3	Continue From Day 2
4	Make Pile for Items That Will Be Tailored
5	Purchase Uniform Hangars & Create Closet System
6	Place Keepers Back in Closet
7	Spend Time with Your Tailor/ Shoe Cobbler

Money Magic
Cash Challenge

Steps	Task
1	Figure out how much cash you need to cover a week's expenses
2	Be honest. Don't deliberately overestimate so that you're sure to have enough cash to get through the week
3	Set the anticipated amount aside and don't use debit or credit cards

Bosswoman Challenge
Boost Your Career

Day	Task
1	Join Glassbreakers
2	Take Your Boss To Lunch To Discuss New Projects to Take On & Career Path
3	Sign up/Attend Next Young Professional Mixer & Email New Contacts
4	Join Professional Networking Group
5	Eat Lunch in Breakroom with Someone You Do Not Know
6	Update Your Resume
7	Enroll in a Continuing Education Course

Contacts Challenge
Connect With Friends

Day	Task
1	Contact a friend you lost touch with this year
2	Contact a friend who lost touch last year
3	Meet a friend for brunch
4	Apologize to a friend
5	Plan a group outing or GNO
6	Have a phone or facebook chat with a long lost relative
7	Plan an outing with a family member

Love Story
Dating Challenge

Day	Task
1	Download a dating app and set it up and leave it alone. No swiping
2	Do something new that you never tried. Maybe a group exercise class at your gym.
3	You can finally swipe for only 10 minutes
4	Do another new activity. Maybe a professionals group event
5	Plan a group outing or GNO
6	Check out your matches and setup times to meet for next week.
7	Confirm your dates for next week.

Here's a tip: If the guy does not respond in a week - DELETE HIM!

Ask Believe Receive
Gratitude List

Day	Task
1	What do you care about the most?
2	What are your most proud of
3	Name 3 people you are thankful for?
4	What are two things that made you smile today?
5	Five physical abilities you are thankful for.
6	What small blessing are you thankful for?
7	Ten things in life you are thankful for.

Sources

Chapter 1: #Mirror Mirror

Print:

Brown, Bobbi. Bobbi Brown Makeup Manual: For Everyone from Beginner to Pro. New York: Springboard Press, 2008

Online:

Pergament, Danielle. "The Allure Aging Survey." http://www.allure.com/beauty-trends/2013/the-allure-aging-survey#slide=1

"Wrinkles In-Depth Report." New York Times. 2008. http://www.nytimes.com/health/guides/symptoms/wrinkles/print.html.

Shah, Yagana. "Everything You Know About Wrinkles Is Wrong." The Huffington Post. http://www.huffingtonpost.com/2014/03/17/wrinkles-and-aging-_n_4919528.html.

"How to Read the New Sunscreen Labels." How to Read the New Sunscreen Labels. https://www.aad.org/public/spot-skin-cancer/learn-about-skin-cancer/prevent/

sunscreen-labels/how-to-read-the-new-sunscreen-labels.

"Skin Cancer Foundation." Skin Cancer Facts.. http://www.skincancer.org/skin-cancer-information/skin-cancer-facts. "Ingredients to Avoid in Hair Products.

Ingredients to Avoid in Hair Products." LIVESTRONG.COM. 2015. http://www.livestrong.com/article/171916-ingredients-to-avoid-in-hair-products/.

Chapter 2: #HeyGoodLooking!

Print:

Budig, Kathryn. The Women's Health Big Book of Yoga. New York, NY: Rodale, 2012.

Online:

"Health and Wellness Tips for Your 30s - Mehmet Oz." Oprah.com. http://www.oprah.com/health/Health-and-Wellness-Tips-for-Your-30s-Mehmet-Oz#ixzz3uYRIEZk3.

8 Reasons Women Should Lift Weights." Bodybuilding.com. 2014.. http://www.bodybuilding.com/fun/8-reasons-women-should-lift-weights.html.

"How The GGS Community Is Changing The Conversation In The Fitness Industry," https://www.girlsgonestrong.com.

"Oprah & Deepak, Become What You Believe https://chopracentermeditation.com/.

Reporter, Daily Mail. "Secrets of an A-list Body: How to Get Courteney Cox's Arms." Mail Online. 2014. http://www.dailymail.co.uk/health/article-2633106/Secrets-A-list-body-How-Courteney-Coxs-arms.html#ixzz3wEQHVTZB.

"Jillian Michaels' No. 1 Workout Trick for Results." Shape Magazine. http://www.shape.com/blogs/fit-famous/jillian-michaels-no-1-trick-maximize-your-workout.

"Victoria's Secret Angels' Legs Workout." - Body Soul. http://www.bodyandsoul.com.au/fitness/work-outs/victorias secret angels legs workout,20625Meet Up.

http://meetup.com.

Study: Looking down at Your Phone Is Ruining Your Spine. http://www.ajc.com/news/news/health-med-fit-science/study-looking-down-your-phone-ruining-your-spine/njCr4/.

Breslau, Ellen. "5 Reasons Your Body Shape Changes As You Age." Huff/Post 50. July 23, 2015.. http://www.huffingtonpost.com/entry/5-reasons-your-body-shape-changes-as-you-age_us_55a808cbe4b0896514d0b2c7.

20 Things All Couples Should Do Before Getting Pregnant." Parents.com.. http://www.parents.com/getting-pregnant/pre-pregnancy-health/general/before-getting-pregnant/#page=6.

Chapter 3: #ChowTime

Print:

Hartwig, Dallas, and Melissa Hartwig. It Starts with Food. Las Vegas: Victory Belt Pub., 2012.

Online:

"Study Finds More Evidence Coffee Can Be a Life-Saver." NBC News. http://www.nbcnews.com/health/health-news/study-finds-more-evidence-coffee-can-be-life-saver-n464386.

"Water Works." Snopes.. http://www.snopes.com/medical/myths/8glasses.asp.

Gregoire, Carolyn. "This Is What Sugar Does To Your Brain." The Huffington Post. http://www.huffingtonpost.com/2015/04/06/sugar-brain-mental-health_n_6904778.html.

"Eat Your Medicine: Food as Pharmacology-Dr. Mark Hyman." Dr Mark Hyman. 2011. http://drhyman.com/blog/2011/10/14/eat-your-medicine-food-as-pharmacology/.

"This Is Your Brain on Sugar: UCLA Study Shows High-fructose Diet Sabotages Learning, Memory." UCLA Newsroom. http://newsroom.ucla.edu/releases/this-is-your-brain-on-sugar-ucla-233992.

Chapter 4: #StyleMe

Print:

Taggart, Judie, and Jackie Walker. I Don't Have a Thing to Wear: The Psychology of Your Closet. New York: Pocket, 2003.

Freer, Alison. How to Get Dressed: A Costume Designer's Secrets for Making Yourclothes Look, Fit, and Feel Amazing.

KonMari and Cathy Hirano, The Life-changing Magic of Tidying Up: The Japanese Art of Decluttering and Organizing. 2014.

Online:

"Super Steamer." SheKnows. 2012 http://www.sheknows.com/home-and-gardening/articles/971625/get-that-dry-cleaned-look-at-home-steam-your-clothes-to-perfection.

"Dress Your Age: Fashion For Women In Their 30's." Indian Fashion Blog with Latest Trends for Women – FashionLady. 2015.

Blalock, Meghan. "25 Items You Definitely Need To Toss By Age 30." Who What Wear. N.p., June-July 2014.

"The Link Between Clothing Choices and Emotional States." GoodTherapy.org Therapy Blog. 2012. http://www.goodtherapy.org/blog/link-between-clothing-choices-and-emotional-states-0330124.

Chapter 5: #MoneyMagic

Print:

Ramsey, Dave. The Total Money Makeover: A Proven Plan for Financial Fitness. Nashville: Thomas Nelson Pub., 2003

Hill, Catey. Shoo, Jimmy Choo!: The Modern Girl's Guide to Spending Less and Saving More. New York, NY: Sterling, 2010

Orman, Suze. Women & Money: Owning the Power to Control Your Destiny. New York: Spiegel & Grau, 2007.

Online:

http://www.Mr MoneyMustache.com

"Future Of Social Security Bleak: Will Congress Save It? | Bankrate.com." Future Of Social Security Bleak: Will Congress Save It? | Bankrate.com.. http://www.bankrate.com/finance/retirement/future-of-social-security.aspx.

Forbes. http://www.forbes.com/sites/nextavenue/2014/11/12/how-the-gender-pay-gap-harms-womens-retirement/.

"Women and Social Security Benefits - AARP." AARP. http://www.aarp.org/work/social-security/info-2014/women-and-social-security-benefits.html.

Chapter 6: #Bosswoman

Print:

Amoruso, Sophia. #GirlBoss. Penguin Books Ltd.2014.

Vanderkam, Laura. What the Most Successful People Do before Breakfast: And Two Other Short Guides to Achieving More at Work and at Home.

Black, Cathie. Basic Black: The Essential Guide for Getting Ahead at Work (and in Life). New York: Crown Business, 2007.

Bryant, Adam. Quick and Nimble: Lessons from Leading CEOs on How to Create a Culture of Innovation.

Online:

Kjerulf, Alexander. "5 Ways Hating Your Job Can Ruin Your Health (According to Science)." The Huffington Post. http://www.huffingtonpost.com/alexander-kjerulf/happiness-tips_b_5001073.html.

"'A Man Wouldn't': What Women Need to Know About Negotiating Salary." 'A Man Wouldn't': What Women Need to Know About Negotiating Salary.. http://www.payscale.com/career-news/2015/02/'a-man-wouldn't'-what-women-need-to-know-about-negotiating-salary.

6 Tips to a Successful Mentorship Forbes. http://www.forbes.com/sites/johnhall/2012/12/18/6-tips-to-a-successful-mentorship/.Mentorship for the modern women

https://www.glassbreakers.co/personal

Chapter 7: #Contacts

Print:

Carnegie, Dale. How to Win Friends and Influence People. New York: Simon and Schuster, 1981

Boothman, Nicholas. How to Make People like You in 90 Seconds or Less. New York: Workman Pub., 2000.

Online:

"5 Ways to Maintain Lifelong Friendships." Psychology Today. https://www.psychologytoday.com/blog/compassion-matters/201301/5-ways-maintain-lifelong-friendships.

Chapter 7: #LoveStory

Print:

Ford, Judy. Single: The Art of Being Satisfied, Fulfilled, and Independent. Avon, MA: Adams Media, 2004

Behrendt, Greg, and Amiira Ruotola-Behrendt. It's Called a Break-up Because It's Broken: The Smart Girl's Break-up Buddy. London: Element, 2005

Stanger, Patti, and Lisa Johnson. Mandell. Become Your Own Matchmaker: 8 Easy Steps for Attracting Your Perfect Mate. New York: Atria Books, 2009.

Online:

Bennett, Jessica. "I'm Not Mad. That's Just My RBF." The New York Times. 2015. http://www.nytimes.com/2015/08/02/fashion/im-not-mad-thats-just-my-resting-b-face.html?_r=0

Samakow, Jessica. "'Ghosting:' The 21st-Century Dating Problem Everyone Talks About, But No One Knows How To Deal With." The Huffington Post.. http://www.huffingtonpost.com/2014/10/30/ghosting-dating-_n_6028958.html.

Chapter 8:#AskBelieveReceive

Print:

Byrne, Rhonda. The Secret. New York: Atria, 2006.

Abraham, Esther Hicks, and Jerry Hicks. The Law of Attraction: The Basics of the Teachings of Abraham. Carlsbad, CA: Hay House, 2006.

Dyer, Wayne W. Wishes Fulfilled: Mastering the Art of Manifesting. Carlsbad, CA: Hay House, 2012.

Sincero, Jen. You are A Badass: How to Stop Doubting Your Greatness and Start Living an Awesome Life, Running Press, 2013

Online:

"Soul Searching? 4 Ways To Uncover Your Truth." Mindbodygreen.2015.http://www.mindbodygreen.com/0-20547/soul-searching-4-ways-to-uncover-your-truth.html.

Live The Book:

Online:

"7-Day Morning Workout Challenge." Skinny Ms. 2015. http://skinnyms.com/7-day-morning-workout-challenge/.

About The Authors

Libby John was born and raised in Houston, Texas. She graduated from Texas A&M University in College Station and is a proud Aggie Engineer, with her PMP (Project Management Professional). Libby is also an RYT-200 Certified Yoga Teacher. Libby loves to read all the latest bestsellers. Her motto in life is Carpe Diem .

Jillian Kaiser is from Houston, Texas, and currently lives in West Palm Beach, Florida, where she works as a Real-Time Power Trader. She has extensive experience in being a woman in her early thirties, and this is her first book on the topic. Her favorite hobbies include tasting and blogging about cheese, volunteering, and traveling abroad. When she is not participating in these activities, she is working on her next writing project to help those with experiences similar to hers become inspired and live their best life.